CAMBRIDGE
UNIVERSITY PRESS

Cambridge
Global English

WORKBOOK 9

Ingrid Wisniewska, Chris Barker, Libby Mitchell & Julie Moore

CAMBRIDGE
UNIVERSITY PRESS

University Printing House, Cambridge CB2 8BS, United Kingdom

One Liberty Plaza, 20th Floor, New York, NY 10006, USA

477 Williamstown Road, Port Melbourne, VIC 3207, Australia

314–321, 3rd Floor, Plot 3, Splendor Forum, Jasola District Centre, New Delhi – 110025, India

103 Penang Road, #05–06/07, Visioncrest Commercial, Singapore 238467

Cambridge University Press is part of the University of Cambridge.

It furthers the University's mission by disseminating knowledge in the pursuit of education, learning and research at the highest international levels of excellence.

www.cambridge.org
Information on this title: www.cambridge.org/9781108963671

First published 2014
Second edition 2022

20 19 18 17 16 15 14 13 12 11 10 9 8 7 6 5 4 3

Printed in India by Multivista Global Pvt Ltd.

A catalogue record for this publication is available from the British Library

ISBN 978-1-108-96367-1 Paperback with Digital Access (1 Year)

Additional resources for this publication at www.cambridge.org/9781108963671

Acknowledgements

The authors and publishers acknowledge the following sources of copyright material and are grateful for the permissions granted. While every effort has been made, it has not always been possible to identify the sources of all the material used, or to trace all copyright holders. If any omissions are brought to our notice, we will be happy to include the appropriate acknowledgements on reprinting.

Unit 3: Extract from *The Summer Book* by Tove Jansson; Extract from *Junko Tabei Masters the Mountains* by Rebel Girls, published by Rebel Girls. Printed by permission. Copyright © 2020 Rebel Girls, Inc.; **Unit 4:** 'Wind on the Hill' from *Now We Are Six* by A.A. Milne. Copyright © Pooh Properties Trust 1927. Reproduced with permissions from Curtis Brown Group Ltd on behalf of The Pooh Properties Trust.; **Unit 5:** Excerpt from *Rickshaw Girl* by Mitali Perkins, copyright © 2007 by Mitali Perkins. Used by permission of Listening Library, an imprint of Penguin Random House LLC. All rights reserved.

Thanks to the following for permission to reproduce images:

Cover Barry Blackman/GI; *Inside* Unit 1 fstop123/GI; Fairfax Media/GI; Gallo Images/GI; Oli Scarff/GI; SolStock/GI; ozgurdonmaz/GI; Kris Gleave/GI; Jason Hosking/GI; LightFieldStudios/GI; Cristian Negroni/GI; izusek/GI; track5/GI; BFG Images/GI; Mehmet Hilmi Barcin/GI; Unit 2 SDI Productions/GI; Carol Yepes/GI; kali9/GI; Deepak Sethi/GI; Ankit Sah/GI; Buena Vista Images/GI; SolStock/GI; betoon/GI; SolStock/GI; Izabela Habur/GI; fStop Images Ivo Gabrowitsch/GI; Unit 3 MyLoupe/GI; Universal History Archive/GI; DEA/Albert Ceolan/GI; Greg Bajor/GI; Nigel Killeen/GI; Mario Tama/GI; Westend61/GI; PEDRE/GI; Kelly Cheng Travel Photography/GI; Unit 4 Yuichiro Chino/GI; janiecbros/GI; Klaus Vedfelt/GI; Sean Russell/GI; Sean White/GI; Michael Leidel/GI; Vicki Jauron, Babylon and Beyond Photography/GI; Nick Dolding/GI; SolStock/GI; SolStock/GI; Olena_T/GI; Anadolu Agency/GI; AleaImage/GI; viktor davare/GI; Unit 5 PixelCatchers/GI; Francois Nascimbeni/GI; fizkes/GI; NurPhoto/GI; Richard Newstead/GI; Alexander Joe/GI; Strauss/Curtis/GI; duncan1890/GI; Sepia Times/GI; DEA/G. Dagli ORTI/GI; Heritage Images/GI; Ed Jones/GI; Ashley Cooper/GI; STR/GI; Marco VDM/GI; Oscar Wong/GI; Peter Dazeley/GI; zhihao/GI; Vladimir Vladimirov/GI; Heritage Images/GI; Unit 6 Phil Boorman/GI; SDI Productions/GI; Miora Rajaonary/GI; Yasser Chalid/GI; Ute Grabowsky/GI; Thomas Koehler/GI; Design Pics/GI; BSR Agency/GI; Justin Sullivan/GI; fstop123/GI; ZU_09/GI; Unit 7 Tim Clayton Corbis/GI; Tetra Images Erik Isakson/GI; Alys Tomlinson/GI; Alex Wong/GI; Brent Lewis/GI; Yasuyoshi Chiba/GI; Justin Tallis/GI; Jun Sato/GI; Unit 8 Roman Studio/GI; Tolga Akmen/GI; JANIFEST/GI; Murat Konac/FOAP/GI; Education Images/GI; The AGE/GI; BrasilNut1/GI; Education Images/GI; Gerard Puigmal/GI; Brandi Mueller/GI; Photos by R A Kearton/GI; Unit 9 Johner Images/GI; VCG/GI; Peter Muller/GI; VCG/GI; PeopleImages/GI; Ker Robertson/GI; tuaindeed/GI; Education Images/GI; Terry Vine/GI

Key: GI= Getty Images

The authors and publishers would like to thank the following for reviewing this Workbook:
Tim Swihart, Mooltripakdee International School.

> Contents

⟩ How to use this book

This Workbook provides questions for you to practise what you have learned in class. There is a unit to match each unit in your Learner's Book, with one page for each lesson.

Tips to help you with your learning. ⟶

Study tip

Before you read an article, look at the headings and any photos or diagrams first. Use the information to predict what is in the text. Ask yourself what you already know about the topic before you start reading.

Information to help you find out more about grammar. ⟶

Use of English

Abstract nouns refer to ideas, qualities or emotions. They are not things that we can see, hear or touch.

General abstract nouns don't need *the*. For example, ***Education*** *is important for children.*

Specific abstract nouns need *the*. *This research is about **the education** of children under 5.*

Many abstract nouns can be formed using these suffixes: *-tion, -ty, -ness, -ism, -dom* and *-ence*.

Use the Cambridge Learner Corpus to get your grammar right! ⟶

Get it right!

Remember to use the correct noun form of these common abstract nouns:

advice, choice, confidence, criticism, development, enjoyment, health, life, organisation, use, work

*The leaflet contains **advice** about healthy eating.* ✓

*The leaflet contains **advise** about healthy eating.* ✗

There are opportunities to practise your grammar on the Use of English pages in each unit. Each Use of English lesson is divided into three parts:

Focus: These grammar questions help you to master the basics.

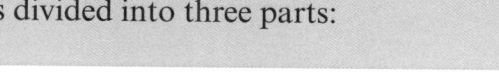

Focus

1   **Choose the correct words.**

   a   We looked for our coach, but he had already *left* / *been left*.

   b   All our money had *spent* / *been spent* on tickets for the final.

   c   They hadn't *won* / *been won* a game for over a year.

   d   Everyone had *given* / *been given* a free ticket to see the game.

   e   He discovered that he had *awarded* / *been awarded* first prize.

   f   She said she hadn't *applied* / *been applied* to enter the competition.

Practice: These grammar questions help you to become more accurate and confident.

Practice

2   **Complete the sentences with the past perfect active or passive of the verb in brackets.**

   a   Sami's uncle .....*had taught*..... (teach) him to play tennis.

   b   They .... (given) new trainers for the match.

   c   How many matches .... (lost) before Saturday's win?

   d   My friends .... (encourage) me to enter the competition.

   e   She .... (tell) she should do more practice if she wanted to win.

Challenge: These questions will help you use language fluently and prepare for the next level.

Challenge

3   **Rewrite the questions or sentences using the past perfect passive.**

   a   They had scored ten goals by the end of the match.

   Ten goals had been scored by the end of the match............................

   b   They hadn't expected him to win the race.

   ....

   c   How many contestants had they interviewed?

   ....

   d   Had they told the fans about the cancellation?

   ....

   e   By half-time, they had sent three players off the field.

   ....

1 ▸ Views and voices

﹥ 1.1 What helps you to learn?

1 **Complete the crossword with words you have used in this lesson.**

Across

2 How often do you ...... with your friends on social media? (4)

4 Do you like to ...... your ideas with other people? (5)

5 What kind of things do students get into ...... for at your school? (7)

6 Do your teachers ...... you to do the very best that you can? (9)

7 Do students in your class sometimes talk when they're not ...... to? (8)

9 Do you sometimes let messages and texts ...... you from your homework? (8)

Down

1 When you ...... classroom learning and online learning, which do you think is better? (7)

2 What helps you to ...... when you are studying alone? (11)

3 Do you think it's always impolite to ...... someone when they are speaking? (9)

8 Do your parents tell you ...... if you get low marks in a test? (3)

2 **In your notebook, answer the questions in the clues with information about yourself.**

Challenge

3 **In your notebook, write a short paragraph about how you learn best. Use the answers to Exercise 2 to help you. Start like this:**

I always listen to music when I'm doing my homework. It helps me to concentrate ...

〉 1.2 Teenage psychology

1 Match the definitions to the correct word from the box.

ambition	communication	~~creativity~~	focus
problem-solving	self-analysis	social flexibility	

a Experimenting with different ways to express your feelings or ideas .... *creativity* ....

b Conversations with other people ....

c Motivation to attempt increasingly more difficult tasks ....

d Ability to adapt to different contexts and environments ....

e Reflecting on your strengths and weaknesses ....

f Ability to concentrate and not get distracted ....

g Looking at an issue from different angles to find the best answer ....

> You're really clever!

> You worked so hard on this project.

2 Imagine that you have just completed a problem-solving task. Which type of praise from the teacher in the photo would you prefer? Why? Write your answer in your notebook.

3 Read the article. Why is it good to have a growth mindset? Answer in your notebook.

> A research study at Columbia University in the US investigated how different types of praise affected students. Psychology professors Mueller and Dweck asked students aged 9 to 12 years old to complete a task. At the end, they praised the students either for their intelligence (the person) or for their hard work (the process). The researchers found that students who were praised for their effort were more likely to ask for feedback on what they had done well and how they could improve. They were more likely to attempt tasks where they could learn new things. The researchers called this a **growth mindset**.

Challenge

4 Which ability in Exercise 1 do you think is most important? In your notebook, suggest three ways you can develop it. Start like this:

I think self-analysis is important because it helps you to ...

> 1.3 Role models

1   **Read about two role models. Which one is similar to your idea of a role model?**

Having a role model is very important to teenagers. A role model can inspire us to be ambitious and follow our dreams. They can help us understand who we want to be when we grow up. They help us overcome obstacles and find our path in life. We asked two teenagers to tell us about their role models.

Sofia, 13
When I was younger, I had lots of different role models. They were usually musicians or actors. I tried to copy their hairstyles and fashions! But now my role model is Malala Yousafzai. I think she was really brave to stand up for what she believes in – which is education for girls. And she risked her life for it! She has a strong sense of justice and shows real leadership. I think she is someone we can all look up to. I'm reading her autobiography at the moment and it's so inspiring!

Jayden, 14
Most of my friends have role models who are athletes or film stars, but for me, a role model is someone who inspires you by their daily life. For me, that person is my grandad. My grandparents came to the UK from Jamaica and started their life here with nothing at all. They built a new life and a strong family. Despite many difficult times, my grandad never gave up. He is always cheerful and kind to others. If I have a problem at school, he is the one I turn to for advice.

2   **Find three things that are the same and three things that are different about these two descriptions.**

Same	Different

3   **Find words in the text that mean the same.**

   a   problems ....

   b   fairness ....

   c   respect ....

   d   courageous ....

   e   ask for help ....

   f   happy ....

❯ *-ing* forms

'Could you stop making so much noise? I need to concentrate on writing my essay. How about reading a book instead of playing that game? Playing here quietly is fine, otherwise you can go outside in the back garden.'

Check!

1 **Read the caption. Underline *-ing* forms after a preposition. Circle *-ing* forms that follow verbs. Draw a dotted line under *-ing* forms that are the subject of a verb.**

2 **Complete the rules.**

We use *-ing* forms:

*   after certain ....¹: *enjoy, hate, finish, mind, stop;*

*   after ....²: *by, for, on, of, about;*

*   as the ....³ of a sentence: ***Managing*** *your time is an important study skill.*

Focus

1 **Circle the correct option to complete the sentences.**

   a   Key vocabulary is worth ***to write / writing*** in your notebook.

   b   At high school, you have to get used to ***do / doing*** things differently.

   c   I prefer to spend time ***reading / to read*** on my own.

   d   ***Share / Sharing*** a room means I don't have a space ***for studying / to studying***.

◎ Get it right!

Remember that some verbs and expressions are followed by a preposition + an *-ing* form. For example:

enthusiastic/excited/shy/worried about + doing

think/wonder about + doing

useful/helpful for/in + doing

thank somebody for + doing

interested in + doing

no point in + doing

succeed in + doing

dream/think of + doing

experience/method of + doing

spend money on + doing

Practice

2 **Are these sentences correct? Put a tick (✓) by the correct sentences. Correct any mistakes in the sentences that are wrong.**

a Good feedback is useful *for/in* ~~to~~ improving your work. ☐

b Some people are only interested to check their grade. ☐

c Everyone has their own method of making notes. ☐

d Some students avoiding answering questions because they're worried to make mistakes. ☐

e It's difficult to choose a career when you have no experience of working. ☐

3 **Choose the correct forms to complete each sentence.**

a I ⟨*make*⟩ / *making* notes on my tablet instead of *write* / ⟨*writing*⟩ them in my book.

b *Study* / *Studying* in a group is a good way to *share* / *sharing* ideas.

c You can *revise* / *revising* for your test by *use* / *using* this new app.

d I really enjoy *do* / *doing* research to *get* / *getting* ideas for my project.

e Do you mind *log* / *logging* in with your password before you *access* / *accessing* the site?

f *Forget* / *Forgetting* my homework can sometimes *get* / *getting* me into trouble.

Challenge

4 **Complete the sentences with the correct preposition from the box and the *-ing* form of the verb in brackets.**

of (×2)	for	from	instead of	~~by~~

a You learn ....*by doing*............ (do).

b I get tired .... (learn) dates in history.

c I sometimes take the bus to school .... (walk).

d I'm not scared .... (ask) questions in class.

e Music doesn't distract me .... (do) my homework.

f I often get into trouble .... (forget) my book.

› Present simple and present continuous

Use of English

Tennis	✓
Football	✗
Homework	✓
Computer game	✗

Julie plays tennis every day. She doesn't play football.

At the moment, she's doing her homework. She isn't playing a computer game.

Check!

1   Read the caption. Underline the positive verbs. Draw a dotted line under the negative verbs.

2   Complete the rules with words from the box.

future   normal   ~~now~~   temporary

Present continuous

We use the present continuous for things that are happening ....*now*........[1]

and for ....[2] situations. It is also used for fixed arrangements in the ....[3]. It is sometimes used to describe an action that is annoying or happens more than ....[4].

Focus

1   **Complete the sentences with one word in each gap.**

a   Zoe usually .....*goes*..... to school by bus. She .... go by bike.

b   We .... playing tennis this term. We're .... badminton instead.

c   .... your sister go to our school? Yes, she ....

d   Are they .... TV right now? No, they ....

e   My brother .... always complaining about having too much homework. He .... have enough time to do it all.

f   Where are you .... for lunch today? I .... going home for lunch.

Practice

2 **Complete the sentences using the present simple or present continuous form of the verb in brackets.**

a Of course, I only know her from the TV, but she ....*seems*........ (seem) really friendly.

b Obviously, I .... (not have) as much money to spend on clothes as my oldest sister.

c My role models are people who

.... (actively do)

things to improve the world.

d It's important for teenagers to see people who .... (look) like them doing different types of jobs.

e I really look up to my father, but he .... (work) abroad at the moment, so I don't see him much.

> ### 🄌 Get it right!
>
> Remember that verbs that express a state (be, have, seem, look), a feeling (want, need) or a belief (understand, know, remember) are usually used in simple not continuous forms.
>
> *We all have people we look up to and admire.* ✓
>
> *We are all having people we look up to and admire.* ✗

3 **Circle the correct options to complete the messages.**

✉ Reply   Forward

I get / I'm getting[1] in touch to ask about the book signing on Saturday. What time *does the event start / is the event starting*[2]? Also, *is the ticket price including / does the ticket price include*[3] a free copy of the book?

📶   100% ▭

What *do you do / are you doing*[4] next Friday? My brother *is having / has*[5] a spare ticket to the tennis championships. He asked me, but I'm not really bothered and I know *you're loving / you love*[6] tennis. *I send / I'm sending*[7] a link with more details. Let me know!

Challenge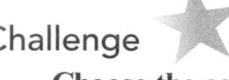

4 **Choose the correct option. Then answer the questions with information about you in your notebook.**

a What time *do you get up* / *are you getting up* every day?

b How often *does your teacher give / is your teacher giving* you homework?

c What *do you wear / are you wearing* today?

d What *do you do / are you doing* when you feel bored?

> 1.4 Teenage voices

1 **Change the underlined word into an adjective to complete each sentence.**

a He helps to take <u>care</u> of his grandparents at home. He's very ....*caring*........

b She doesn't mind taking <u>responsibility</u> for her younger brother. She's very

....

c He tends to <u>defy</u> his parents if they tell him what do to. He's very ....

d I generally <u>rebel</u> against any kind of authority. I'm quite ....

e He <u>disobeys</u> some of the rules. He's very ....

f He doesn't <u>care</u> if he makes mistakes in his work. He's very ....

g She doesn't <u>respect</u> the opinions of older people. She's quite ....

Dictionary work

Using a dictionary to find word families (words from the same root) can help you improve your vocabulary.

> **obey** (verb)   do what someone tells you to do; **obedient** (adjective) / **obedience** (noun); **disobedient** (adjective) / **disobedience** (noun)

2 **Write the correct form of two adjectives from Exercise 1 next to each person.**

 **Tariq:** I think I'm sometimes angry with everyone because I want to develop my own identity.

...........*rebellious*..........., ...

 **Chang:** I usually visit my grandmother after school so she doesn't feel lonely.

...................., ...

 **Zoe:** I say what I think and I don't care if I hurt people's feelings.

...................., ...

 **Jack:** I try to be a good role model for my younger brother and always look out for him.

...................., ...

Challenge

3 **Which adjectives describe you? Explain why. Write a short paragraph in your notebook.**

You could start like this: *I think I am …*

› 1.5 Facts and opinions

1 **Read the descriptions and complete them with words from the box.**

arrested	~~demonstration~~	demonstrators	issue
march	marched	placards	protesters

Many young people took part in a …*demonstration*…[1] in London last Friday. The …………………[2] was peaceful and kept to one side of the road so that traffic could continue. Many …………………[3] carried …………………[4] with slogans such as: 'There's no planet B' because they are all worried about one …………………[5] and that is climate change.

A group of angry …………………[6] flooded the streets of London last Friday. They …………………[7] angrily down the street, disrupting traffic and causing noise and confusion. Several people were …………………[8] by police.

2 **Answer the questions.**

a Why do you think people take part in demonstrations?

…………………………………………………………………………………………

b Why do you think these people are worried about climate change?

…………………………………………………………………………………………

c What do you think the slogan 'There is no planet B' means?

A We need to find another planet.

B We shouldn't look for planet B.

C We must save this planet.

Challenge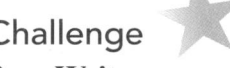

3 **Write your own slogan for a poster about climate change.**

…………………………………………………………………………………………

〉 1.6 From ideas into words

1 Complete the conversation between two friends. What does Yasmin say to Sylvie?
For questions a–f, write the correct number 1–6.

Sylvie: Can you help me with preparing
my presentation?

Yasmin: a ....

Sylvie: I'm working on them right now.
Can I show them to you?

Yasmin: b ....

Sylvie: OK. How does this look?

Yasmin: c ....

Sylvie: Do you mean some photos or drawings?

Yasmin: d ....

Sylvie: Good idea. Is there anything else
I can do?

Yasmin: e ....

Sylvie: To get the audience involved right from
the start?

Yasmin: f ....

1 Of course. Have you made some
slideshow slides?

2 Starting with an image or a
question is often a good idea.

3 That looks good. You could
also add some visuals to make
it more interesting.

4 That's right. Why don't we
brainstorm some ideas together?

5 Yes, let's take a look. You
shouldn't put too much text on
each slide.

6 Yes, you can search for them
in the image bank or on the
internet.

2 Read the conversation again. Underline an example of a way to:

a	make a suggestion	**c**	make sure you understand	**e**	ask for an opinion
b	ask for advice	**d**	give praise	**f**	accept a suggestion

Challenge

3 Think about your last class presentation. What did you do well? What did you need
to improve? Circle the correct option and write notes to yourself in your notebook.

• I *used plenty of / didn't use enough* visuals.

• I put *too much / the right amount of* text on each slide.

• I *did enough / didn't do enough* practice.

• I *was / wasn't* nervous.

• I had *too much / just the right amount of* material.

> Present simple passive

Use of English

Check!

1 **Underline the passive words in each sentence. What is the auxiliary verb? What is the main verb? What form is the main verb?**

Lucia: Why are we always told off for wasting time or for not working hard enough? It's not fair.

Nila: I agree. We aren't given enough free time to hang out with our friends and have fun!

2 **Complete the rules with words from the box.**

between	~~know~~	object	past	subject

We use the passive when we don't ....*know*.......¹ who did or said something, or if it isn't important or if it is really obvious.

We form the present simple passive by using the verb *be* followed by the ....² participle.

The object of an active sentence becomes the ....³ of a passive sentence.

Adverbs of frequency go ....⁴ the auxiliary and the participle.

We cannot use the passive with verbs that don't have an ....⁵, for example *arrive, live.*

Focus

1 **Complete these sentences using the present simple passive of the verbs in brackets.**

a I *'m often told*............ that I am quite creative and funny. (often, tell)

b Teens .... to spend too much time on screens. (usually, think)

c .... students in your school .... time to study on their own without a teacher? (sometimes, give)

d .... children .... for their opinions? (usually, not ask)

e My brother says that he .... (often, misunderstand)

f .... I .... to make decisions about what to study? (generally, expect)

Practice

2 **Complete the sentences using the modal verb and the present simple passive form of the verb in brackets.**

a Young people ...*should be given*... (should / give) more freedom to make their own choices.

b Nowadays, people .... (can / contact) 24/7 via their mobile phones.

c There are still some jobs that .... (can / not / do) by machines.

d Your desk at home .... (should / keep) tidy and organised.

e Some classes .... (may / affect) by timetable changes, so please check the website.

f Remember that art classes .... (must / always / book) in advance.

g Simple changes .... (can / easily / make) to make the room accessible to disabled people.

 **Get it right!**

Remember that we sometimes use a modal verb with a present simple passive: *can/ should + be +* past participle.

This technology **can be used** *for all kinds of purposes.* ✓

This technology can used for all kinds of purposes. ✗

The lights **should be turned off** *when the classroom's empty.*

Challenge

3 **Complete the paragraph with the present simple active or passive forms of verbs from the box.**

choose	complete	emphasise	encourage	give
lose	not finish	say	spend	~~tell~~

I'm really enjoying lessons at my new school. I'*m told* ....¹ that maths and science are my strongest subjects. In our maths lessons, we ....² a lot of challenging problems to solve. Our teacher ....³ that it's important to learn to work in groups. Problem-solving and communication skills ....⁴ a lot in our lessons. We ....⁵ to take responsibility for our studies. One task is that each of us ....⁶ a project, which must ....⁷ by the end of the term. It's up to us how much time we ....⁸ on it. If it ....⁹ or if it is late, we ....¹⁰ marks.

〉 Present continuous passive

Use of English

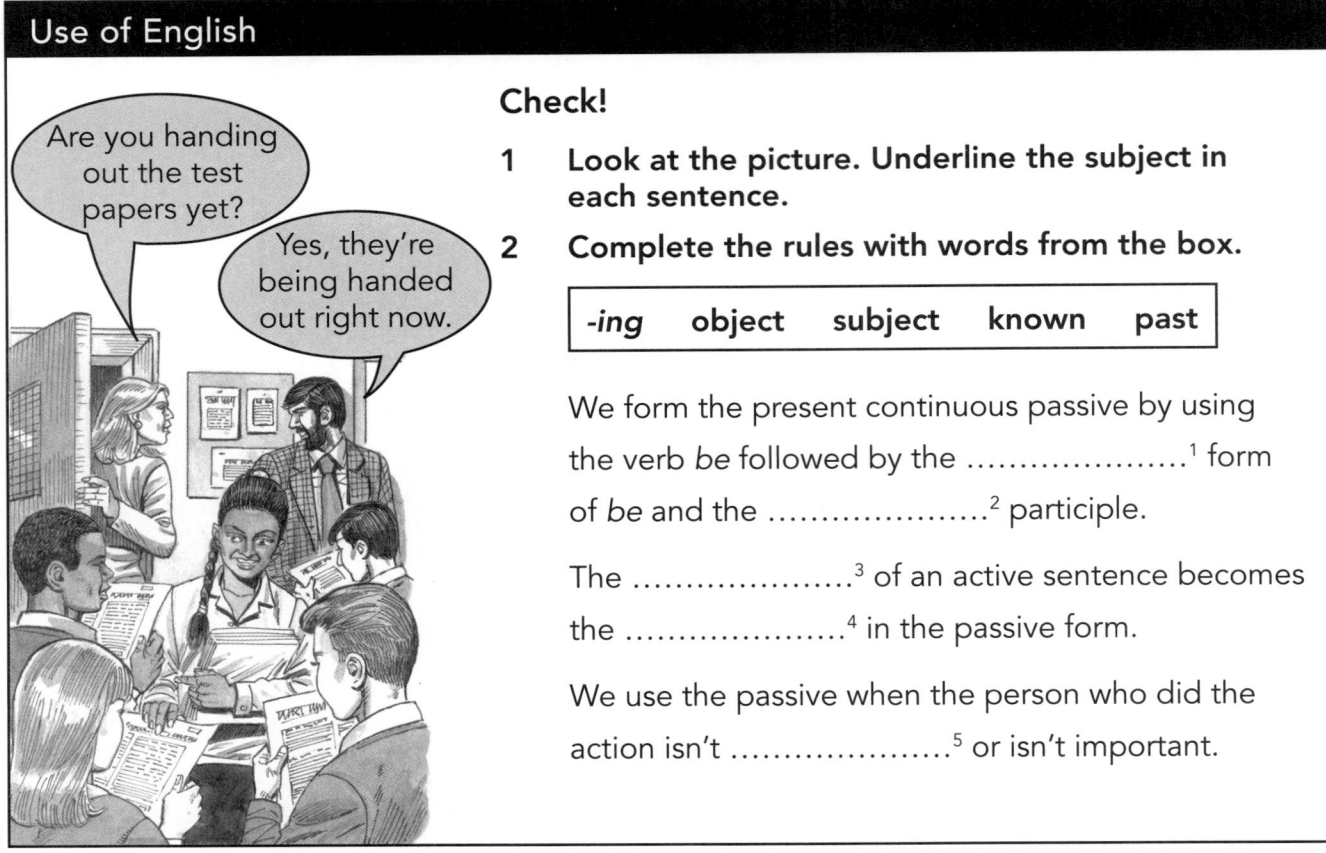

Are you handing out the test papers yet?

Yes, they're being handed out right now.

Check!

1   Look at the picture. Underline the subject in each sentence.

2   Complete the rules with words from the box.

| *-ing* | object | subject | known | past |

We form the present continuous passive by using the verb *be* followed by the ....[1] form of *be* and the ....[2] participle.

The ....[3] of an active sentence becomes the ....[4] in the passive form.

We use the passive when the person who did the action isn't ....[5] or isn't important.

Focus

1   Complete the sentences using the present continuous passive of the word in brackets.

a   We' .re being given......... (give) extra homework today.

b   The school assembly .... (hold) in the main hall.

c   The computers .... (not repair) until tomorrow.

d   Money .... (collect) to buy new school sports equipment.

e   Students .... (tell) whether they have passed the exam.

f   The decision .... (not make) by our teacher, it's by all of the teachers.

Practice

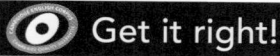 **Get it right!**

Remember that in questions, we place the first auxiliary verb (*am, is* or *are*) after the question word (wh- questions) or as the first word (yes/no questions). The second auxiliary verb (*being*) stays with the past participle.

Why **are** we being followed? ✓   Why we **are** being followed? ✗

Is the car being repaired? ✓   *Is being the car repaired?* ✗

2   Correct the mistake in each sentence.

    a   Some new students are ~~be~~ *being* interviewed.

    b   A new gym is being build next to our school.

    c   The windows are being wash today.

    d   Are being our books delivered this afternoon?

    e   Where the tickets are being sold?

    f   These computers isn't being used by anyone.

Challenge

3   Complete the sentences using the present continuous passive form of verbs in the box.

deliver	~~clean~~	not use	paint	put on hold	watch

    a   I can't wear my jacket because it ....*is being cleaned*...........

    b   You can study in this classroom because it ....

    c   We don't have to pick up the tickets because they ....

    d   Can you see the camera on that wall? I think we ....

    e   No one is answering the phone so I ....

    f   There are ladders all over the building because it ....

> 1.7 Improve your writing

1 Complete the sentences with suitable words from the box.

> advance   appreciate   hearing
> reason   well   wonder

a Hello Lily! I hope you and your family are ....

b The .... I'm writing is to ask you for some help.

c I .... if you could help me by answering these questions.

d I'd really .... your help with this.

e Thank you in ....!

f Looking forward to .... from you.

2 Number the sentences in the best order for an introduction to an informal email.

a [ ] Anyway, I'd like to ask you a favour …

b [ ] Are you still doing <u>karate</u>?

c [ ] Have you been very busy with <u>schoolwork</u>?

d [1] Hi <u>Monica</u>,

e [ ] How are you?

f [ ] I haven't heard from you for <u>ages</u>.

g [ ] I often think about you and about our <u>summer holiday together last year</u>.

3 Rewrite the email introduction in the correct order and change the underlined words so that they are about your friend.

Challenge

4 Choose one of the following topics for a project. In your notebook, add a paragraph to your email in Exercise 3 asking your friend three questions about the topic.

• Role models for teenagers

• Teenage life

• Teenage stereotypes

> 1.8 Autobiography

1 **Read the sentences from an autobiography.**
Which question does each one answer?

.....C..... What is your earliest memory?

.... What was your bedroom like when you
were younger?

.... What was your best holiday experience?

.... What were you like when you were younger?

.... Who has had the biggest influence on your life?

[ ] **A** When I was 5 or 6 years old, I was quite shy and
quiet, but now I'm more sociable and talkative.

[ ] **B** I can see my bedroom from when I was 8 years old.
Everything is purple! The cushions, the bed cover,
the curtains and even the lampshade! And there
are posters of my favourite pop stars on the wall.

[ ] **C** The first thing I remember in my life is waking
up in my pram in the back garden and seeing an
enormous butterfly sitting on my blanket.

[ ] **D** An important influence in my life has been my
older sister. She always helped me at school and
encouraged me to do my best.

[ ] **E** The best holiday I've ever had was when we went scuba diving in
Mexico last year. The colours of the fish and the coral were truly
unforgettable. I want to be an underwater photographer one day!

2 **Number the questions chronologically from the past to the present.**

3 **Answer the questions from Exercise 1 about yourself and make notes.**
Use your notes to write your own autobiography in your notebook.

....

....

....

....

....

2 ▶ Well-being

> 2.1 Food for health

1 **Put the letters in the correct order to complete the sentences.**

a If you don't eat meat, you are ......*vegetarian*....... . (gaenteriva)

b Burgers, French fries and pizza are examples of .... (saft odof)

c When people don't have enough food, they can suffer from .... (ilnamtutorin)

d The energy value of food is measured in the number of .... (rolcisae)

e .... is usually high in fat and sugar. (knuj dofo)

f If children don't eat enough healthy food, they can become .... (derun-ideshurno)

g The average teenager .... about 2,000 calories per day. (musnoces)

h For people who don't eat a healthy diet and don't exercise regularly, ... can be a problem. (soybite)

i If you let food go bad in the fridge, it is an example of .... (sweta doof)

j Eating a variety of vegetables and fruit as well as wholegrains is an example of a .... diet. (danalceb)

Challenge ⭐

2 **Write a personal food diary in your notebook. Use the following questions to help you.**

How much or how many of each type of food do you eat every day? How do you want to improve your diet? What do you want to eat more of or less of?

Write three sentences that are true for you.

I eat a lot of fruit, but I don't eat many vegetables.

❯ 2.2 Food for thought

1   **Complete the text with words from the box.**

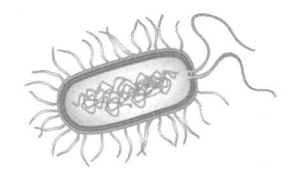

~~bacteria~~	cells	diabetes	disease
immune system	infections	recovery	viruses

........*Bacteria*........¹ are small organisms that can live on surfaces or inside our body. They are made up of single small ....². Most of them do not cause any harm. Some can cause ....³, such as food poisoning. They can be treated with antibiotics, which usually lead to a complete ....⁴.

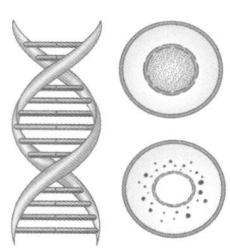

..........................⁵ are much smaller than bacteria. Once they enter your body, they start to reproduce and attack different organs. Vaccination helps to prepare the body's ....⁶ to fight the disease. Colds and flu are usually caused by viral infections.

..........................⁷ is a disease that occurs when the body isn't able to regulate blood sugar levels in the body. People with this illness need to test their blood sugar regularly and take medicine. Eating a healthy diet and exercising regularly are two ways to prevent this ....⁸.

2   **Link the causes a–e with the effects 1–5.**

a	Bacteria .....*3*.....		**1**	Colds and flu
b	Antibiotics		**2**	Irregular blood sugar levels
c	Viruses		**3**	Food poisoning
d	Vaccinations		**4**	Recovery from bacterial infections
e	Diabetes		**5**	Stronger immune system

3   **Number the conversation in the correct order.**

[ ] **Mei:**   Is that because you have more energy?

[ ] **Mei:**   It's true that I'm usually in a bad mood if I skip breakfast!

[ ] **Mei:**   Oh, I skipped breakfast – I was a bit late.

[ ] **Aisha:**   That's not good. You need to eat breakfast to do well at school.

[*1*] **Aisha:**   What did you have for breakfast this morning?

[ ] **Aisha:**   Yes, it helps your brain to concentrate better and it also improves your mood.

4   **Write a similar conversation in your notebook about doing regular exercise.**

› 2.3 Are you getting enough sleep?

1 **Read the letters. What are both people worried about?** ....

Are you having health problems? Ask Auntie Ana for advice!

Dear Auntie Ana,

I'm constantly exhausted during the day, but when it's time to go to bed I don't feel sleepy. I start to worry about things that happened during the day and it's hard for me to relax. I wake up quite often during the night and can't get back to sleep, so I end up checking my emails and texts, and looking at websites. What can I do to get a good night's sleep?

Tania

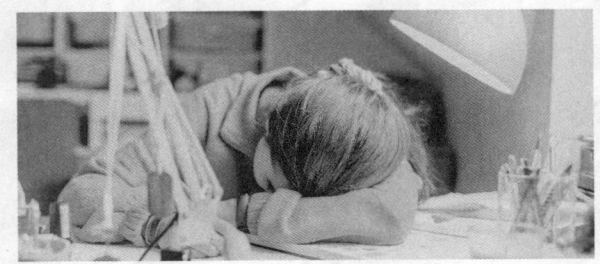

Dear Auntie Ana,

I often play games on my computer in the evening before going to sleep. Sometimes I play for several hours and when I look at the clock it's already 2 a.m. Then, when the alarm goes off at 7 in the morning, it's really hard for me to get up. Sometimes I have to skip breakfast because I'm so late. Sometimes I forget to brush my hair. I'd like to spend less time on games, but once I start playing I can't stop! Do you think this is a cause for concern? Can you give me some advice?

Kemal

2 **Match the advice a–h with the person from Exercise 1.**
Write the correct letters in the chart.

a It's a good idea to banish technology from your bedroom.

b You could be at risk of anxiety and depression.

c Calm music promotes a relaxing environment.

d You can lose track of time when you play computer games.

e Breathing exercises can help you to wind down.

f It's important to take care of your appearance.

g Checking your phone during the night isn't a good idea.

h Not getting enough sleep can affect your health.

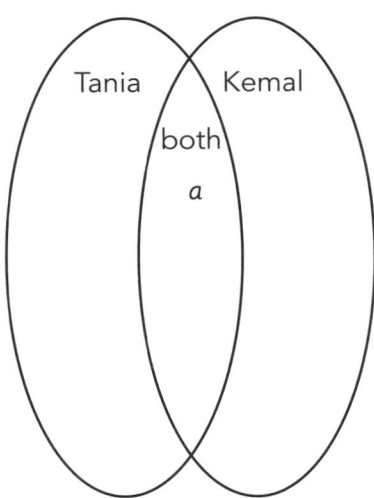

Tania   Kemal
both
a

Challenge

3 **Choose one of the letters to Auntie Ana and write a reply in your notebook giving some advice. Include some sentences from Exercise 2.**

〉 Abstract nouns

Abstract nouns refer to ideas, qualities or emotions. They are not things that we can see, hear or touch.

General abstract nouns don't need *the*. For example, **Education** *is important for children.*

Specific abstract nouns need *the*. *This research is about* **the education** *of children under 5.*

Many abstract nouns can be formed using these suffixes: *-tion, -ty, -ness, -ism, -dom* and *-ence.*

Check!

Underline the abstract nouns in the picture.

The development of the human brain

How do nutrition and exercise affect the human brain?

Focus

1 **Circle the abstract nouns.**

beautiful	(kindness)	develop	scientist
generosity	progress	healthy	nutrition
educator	destruction	exploration	organism

2 **Write the abstract noun for each word.**

a intelligent ....*intelligence*............

b friend ....

c anxious ....

d strong ....

e free ....

f dark ....

Practice

3 **Choose the correct word to complete the sentences.**

a Avoiding food waste at home involves a little bit more planning and *organise /* *~~organisation~~*.

b A *health / healthy* diet is really important for a child's *develop / development*.

c The *use / using* of children's cartoon characters to advertise sugary foods has brought *criticise / criticism* from doctors.

d A doctor has to feel *confidence / confident* they are giving the best *advice / advise*.

e The *work / working* of the charity helps these children to lead a more active *life / live*.

Challenge

4 **Underline the abstract nouns. Add *the* if necessary.**

a Teenagers often underestimate $\overset{the}{\underset{\wedge}{\underline{importance}}}$ of getting enough sleep.

....

b There is a link between nutrition and doing well at school.

....

c Nutritional value of junk food is usually quite low.

....

d Climate change is going to cause food shortages.

....

e Depression and anxiety can be the result of a poor diet.

....

f Risk of eating too much sugar is diabetes.

....

5 **Which of the statements in Exercise 4 do you think are true? Why? Write True or False and why under each statement.**

⊙ Get it right!

Remember to use the correct noun form of these common abstract nouns:

advice, choice, confidence, criticism, development, enjoyment, health, life, organisation, use, work

The leaflet contains **advice** *about healthy eating.* ✓

The leaflet contains **advise** *about healthy eating.* ✗

People have a lot of **choice** *when it comes to food.* ✓

People have a lot of **chose** *when it comes to food.* ✗

Someone's **health** *affects their quality of* **life** ✓

Someone's **healthy** *affects their quality of* **live**. ✗

> Comparative adjectives and adverbs

Use of English

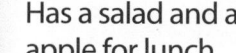

Sofia

Gets up at 6 a.m.

Lives 20 minutes' walk from school

Has a salad and an apple for lunch

Spends 25 minutes eating lunch

Plays volleyball once a week

Nabil

Gets up at 7 a.m.

Lives 10 minutes' walk from school

Has pizza and crisps for lunch

Spends 15 minutes eating lunch

Goes running every day

Sofia gets up earlier than Nabil. Sofia's journey to school is longer than Nabil's. Nabil gets up later than Sofia. Nabil's home is closer to school.

Check!

1   **Look at the pictures. Complete the sentences about Sofia and Nabil.**

Sofia has a ………*healthier*………[1] (healthy) lunch. Sofia eats lunch ………….……………[2] (slow). Sofia is …………….…………..[3] (active) than Nabil.

Nabil's lunch is …………….…………..[4] (healthy) than Sofia's. Nabil eats lunch …………….…………..[5] (quick). Nabil is …………….…………..[6] (active) than Sofia.

2   **Complete the rules with words from the box.**

adjective	adverb	less	long	short

To make comparative adjectives, we add -(e)r to …………….…………..[1] adjectives or use *more* in front of most …………….…………..[2] adjectives.

To make negative comparisons, we use …………….…………..[3] in front of longer adjectives. We can also use *not as . . . as* with any …………….…………..[4] or adverb.

To make comparative adverbs, use *more* and add -*ly* to the …………….…………..[5].

Irregular adjectives: *good – better, bad – worse*
Irregular adverbs: *well – better, badly – worse, far – farther*

Focus

1 **Choose the correct word to complete the sentences.**

a My brother isn't a good swimmer, but I am. I can swim *more well /* *better*.

b Omar doesn't exercise regularly. I exercise more *frequent / frequently* than him.

c Your homework is too difficult. My homework is less *difficult / easier* than yours.

d My sister isn't good at French, but I am. I can speak French more *fluent / fluently* than her.

e We don't get up early at weekends. We get up *more early / earlier* on weekdays.

Practice

2 **Choose the correct option to complete the sentences.**

a After a good night's sleep, you'll be able to think *clearer /* *more clearly /* *more clearer*.

b I hope he'll be *more careful / more carefully / more carefull* next time so he doesn't get injured again.

c She says she can breathe *easier / more easy / more easily* when she gets out of the city.

d When you eat *more slowly / more slower / slower*, you feel full sooner.

e My grandfather looked much *more healthily / healthy / healthier* when I saw him last week.

Challenge

3 **Complete the sentences using the comparative adjective or adverb form of words from the box.**

~~efficient~~	frequent	likely	quick	susceptible

a Maintaining blood sugar levels helps you to work ..... *more efficiently* .....

b Exercising regularly means you are .... to catch a cold.

c People who eat a healthy diet are .... to illness.

d Skipping meals means that you eat snacks ....

e If you do too much exercise when you are ill, you will recover ....

4 **In your notebook, use comparative forms to write three more sentences about how to stay healthy.**

› 2.4 Moods and feelings

1 **How would you feel in these situations? Write the correct adjectives to complete the puzzle.**

   1   You watched a frightening film and all the lights suddenly went out.

   2   Your friend promised to meet you at 3 p.m. today but then sent an email saying 4 p.m.

   3   Your friends have gone away for the weekend and you've got nothing to do.

   4   Your favourite football team won a match against a top team.

   5   Your friend borrowed your phone and damaged the screen.

   6   You're going to go skiing for the first time this winter.

   7   You forgot about your best friend's graduation and didn't send her a present.

2 **Find the mystery word in the puzzle. In your notebook, describe a situation which would make you feel like this.**

⟩ 2.5 Keep a cool head

1   Read the article. Underline four nouns for different emotions.

Emotional intelligence

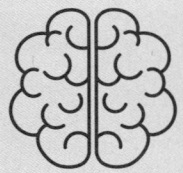

Emotional intelligence is a group of skills that includes the ability to identify and manage one's own emotions and understand the emotions of other people. A person with emotional intelligence can understand their own feelings, of anger or annoyance and how they will affect other people. They know how to stay calm in tense situations. They are also aware of the emotions of those around them and can pick up signals that indicate sadness or happiness. It is thought that a high degree of emotional intelligence is important in leadership roles. A manager, for example, would be able to gain the trust of the team members more easily, would

not shout or get upset, would listen carefully to team members before making a decision and would know how to deal with their emotional responses.

2   Using the article above, tick (✓) the adjectives that describe a person with emotional intelligence.

| ✓ collaborative | ☐ competitive | ☐ empathetic | ☐ indecisive |
| ☐ self-aware | ☐ self-controlled | ☐ sensitive | |

Challenge

3   How can you learn to improve your emotional intelligence? Write three ideas in your notebook.

> ## 2.6 How to be happy

1   **Read Emine's blog about how to be happy. Underline the ideas that you agree with.**

My podcast today is about how to be happy. What are some active strategies for maintaining a positive mindset? I'm going to suggest three ways we can help ourselves to be happy.

[1] First, it's really obvious, but also very true that our health influences our mood. Getting enough sleep, doing regular exercise and eating a balanced diet are all good ways to combat stress and anxiety. [A]

[2] Second, it's good to vary our activities every day. Socialising and getting involved in activities with others is really important. But having time on your own to reflect on things is necessary too. Sometimes we need to concentrate hard on tasks that are quite difficult and other times we need to relax more. [B]

[3] Finally, try to focus on the good things in your daily life. Whether you're with your family or at school, look around you and say what you are grateful for. It can be something small, like a sunny day or getting good marks on a quiz. [C]

Well, that's all from me today. What do you think about how to be happy? Leave a comment!

2   **Where do these sentences go? Write the correct letter, A, B or C.**

.... So a balance of activities throughout the day is super important.

.... If our brains and bodies are rested and well-nourished, we will feel good.

.... Try doing this at least once a day – it can really lift your mood.

3   **Which paragraph mentions the following topics? Write the correct number, 1, 2 or 3. (Two are not mentioned.)**

[ ] Being alone   [ ] Friendship   [ ] Physical well-being   [ ] Bullying

[ ] Being at home   [ ] Bad behaviour   [ ] Getting depressed

Challenge ⭐

4   **Write a summary of the blog in one sentence.**

....

> *must have, might have, can't have* + past participle

Use of English

Check!

Complete the rules.

We use *must / might / can't* + have + past participle to talk about probability in the past.

He .... [1] have lost his phone. (We're certain that it happened.)

He .... [2] have lost his phone. (We aren't certain that it happened.)

He .... [3] have lost his phone. (We are certain that it didn't happen.)

Where's my phone?

Focus

1 **Look at the picture above and write sentences about where the phone might be.**

   a he / drop his phone / at the bus stop.

   ....

   b he / leave his phone on the bus.

   ....

   c he / leave his phone at school.

   ....

   d Dad: That was a new phone! You / lose / it already!

   ....

Practice

2 Correct the mistakes. Use ^ to add words where you need to.

a There's no ice cream left in the fridge. Someone must ^*have* eaten it.

b Dina is late for our meeting. She might to have missed the train.

c I wasn't at school yesterday. You didn't could have seen me.

d Jason only left about two minutes ago. He can't to have arrived home already.

e I didn't see Marianna at the bus stop. She might got an earlier bus.

f You've finished your lunch already! You must have to be hungry!

Challenge

3 Read the situations and write a sentence using *must / might* or *can't* and the words in brackets.

a Anna studied very hard last term. (pass, English exam)
She must have passed her English exam.

b The ground is wet. (rain, last night)

c Ivan is looking for something under the desk. (drop something)

d Sylvie was absent for two days. (have a cold)

e You didn't eat your lunch. (hungry)

f They're covered in mud. (play football in the rain)

> # Strong adjectives and intensifiers

Use of English

Check!
Complete the rules with words from the box.

| delicious | ~~friendly~~ | highly | really |

Gradable adjectives are words like *big, small,* ......*friendly*......[1], *kind*. These adjectives have different degrees of strength. We can make them stronger or weaker by using them with intensifiers such as *very, a bit* and *extremely, quite* and *rather*.

Strong adjectives are words like *furious,* ....[2], *hilarious* and *delighted*. These adjectives do not have different degrees of strength, but we can make them stronger by using them with intensifiers such as *absolutely, completely, extremely, highly, particularly, really* and *totally*.

Some intensifiers go with particular words. For example, ...[3] tends to go with *likely/unlikely, unusual, successful, intelligent, susceptible* and *competitive*. ....[4] can go with any type of adjective.

> Was your dad angry about his windscreen being broken?

> He wasn't just angry. He was absolutely furious!

Focus

1 **Circle the strong adjectives.**

amazing	angry	bad	big	delicious	delighted	enormous
funny	furious	good	happy	hilarious	hungry	miserable
sad	small	starving	tasty	terrible	tiny	

Practice

Get it right!

Remember these common intensifier + adjective combinations:

- Communication is **absolutely essential** in a relationship.
- Are you **absolutely sure** you want to leave?
- We're **not entirely sure** why it happens.
- We had a **really great** time.

Different can go with a wide range of intensifiers: *completely / totally / entirely / very / slightly / quite.*

- The two brothers are **completely different.**
- They have **very different** personalities.
- Each house in the street is **slightly different.**

2   Match the sentence halves.

a   Hannah is completely

b   A warm coat is absolutely

c   The family had to get used to a totally

d   They're not exactly

e   Everyone gave a slightly

1   different version of what happened.

2   essential in the winter.

3   sure she closed the door.

4   different way of life.

5   sure when it will open again.

3   Are these sentences correct? Tick (✓) the correct sentences. Correct any mistakes in the sentences that are wrong.

a   We were all completely disappointed when the trip was cancelled. ☐

b   Everyone found her childish behaviour really annoying. ☐

c   Listen everyone! Arif has some absolutely exciting news. ☐

d   By the end of the day we were all very exhausted. ☐

e   My parents have very different ideas about using social media. ☐

Challenge

4   Choose the correct word.

a   The TV programme was *very /* *absolutely* hilarious.

b   The meal was a *bit / completely* delicious.

c   Their flat is *quite / totally* small.

d   The concert was absolutely *fantastic / good*.

e   This book is totally *interesting / amazing*.

f   The film was very *awful / disappointing*.

⟩ 2.7 Improve your writing

1 **Follow the steps. Read the questions and make notes in your notebook.**

- Look carefully at the photo in the article below. What is the main focus? Where was it taken? Who took the photo? Why?

- Think of some vivid phrases to describe the photo. For example, what kind of adjectives could you use?

- Speculate about what happened before the photo was taken. Think of three or four ideas and choose the best one.

- Speculate on what might happen next. Think of a funny ending for your description.

- Think of a title for your description.

2 **Look at the photo in the article. What do you think is happening? Write one idea.**

....

3 **Read the description. Does it match your idea?**

Computer scientists OF THE FUTURE

The students in the photo are working hard on a computer project. It doesn't look like a normal classroom. It might be some kind of computer science lab. Three students are looking at a computer screen. They are highly focused on their task, while the teacher is watching and observing their work carefully. The students seem to be really excited about the task. It looks like two of the girls are laughing. They might have just solved a problem, or they may have just learned how to use some new kind of computer program. Perhaps they will become highly skilled computer scientists in the future.

4 **What questions does the description answer? Write three questions in your notebook.**

5 **Choose your own photo and write a description in your notebook. Include the underlined phrases in the description. Remember to think of a good title.**

> 2.8 Fiction

1   Read the title of the story. What do you think it will be about? Then read the story and complete the sentences with words from the box.

The fisherman and the fish

boat	hut	nets	sea	talk

Once there was a fisherman who lived in a small wooden ....[1]. He was poor but happy. His only food was the fish that he caught in the ....[2]. One day, he took his ....[3] out and fished all day but caught only one small fish. He pulled in his ....[4] and put the fish into his basket. Suddenly the fish started to ....[5]. 'Please, Mr Fisherman, put me back in the sea!'

back	food	hungry	surprised	without

The fisherman was so ....[6] to see a fish that could talk that at first he couldn't speak at all. He felt sorry for the fish. Then he realised that this was all he had to eat and ....[7] this fish he would be ....[8]. He looked at the fish and said, 'Why should I put you ....[9] in the sea? You will be my only ....[10] today.'

2   How do you think the story will continue? Choose what you think the fish will say next. Add your own idea.

a   'I am so small, it is not worth taking me home. Put me back so I can grow bigger and I'll be a much better meal for you.'

b   'I am not an ordinary fish. I am a prince under a magic spell. If you throw me back into the sea, I will grant you any wish that you want.'

c   'Please have pity on me. I am only a small fish. Put me back in the sea and I will show you where to catch much bigger fish.'

d   ....

3   Think about how to continue the story. Make notes in your notebook. Then write the ending.

•   What kind of man is the fisherman? Is he greedy, suspicious or kind?

•   What does he say to the fish?

•   What happens to the fish and what happens to the fisherman at the end?

3 ▶ Tourism

> 3.1 On holiday

1 Match the words to make compound nouns. Complete the sentences with one word from each box.

~~beach~~	first-aid	hot
picnic	swimming	theme

basket	kit	park
pool	spring	~~umbrella~~

a The sun is very strong. We'd better put up our ...*beach umbrella*.... .

b Last summer we visited Water Fun World, which is a famous

....

c Let's have lunch in the park! I'll put sandwiches and cake into my

....

d I'm going to practise my diving in the ....

e People love to relax in this ....

f I've cut my finger. Can you get me the .... ?

2 Complete the advertisement with words from the box.

boat	campfire	campsite	go	insect	skating	sports	tennis	waterskiing

Are you planning to ....*go*.....¹ camping this summer?
Come to our lovely ....² just three minutes' walk
from a beautiful beach. You can ....³ windsurfing,
try ....⁴ and do many other water ....⁵. You
can go on ....⁶ trips to the islands. There are also two
..............⁷ courts and a park for skateboarding and roller
..............⁸. Join us round the ....⁹ to share food and
sing songs. Just bring a tent, sunscreen and some ....¹⁰
repellent for a holiday you'll never forget.

Challenge ⭐

3 In your notebook, describe a place you would like to go for a picnic or a day trip.
Say what you would like to do there using compound nouns from Exercises 1 and 2.

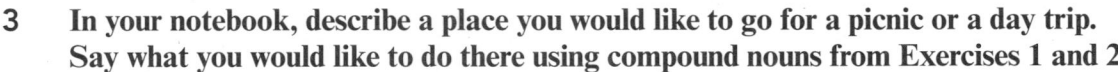

〉 3.2 A holiday to remember

1   Write the words or phrases under the correct photos.

amphitheatre   arches   arena   ~~built in the Roman period~~
castle   frescoes   high walls   built in the Renaissance period
palace   built in the Medieval period

a

b

c

built in the Roman period 1

.... 2

.... 3

.... 4

.... 5

.... 6

.... 7

.... 8

.... 9

.... 10

Challenge ⭐

2   Make notes about what you could see or do in each place.

....
....
....
....

3   Choose one place and write a blog post about your visit.

....
....
....
....

> 3.3 How was your holiday?

1 Read the blog entries a–d. Complete them with multi-word verbs from the box. Use the past tense.

break down	~~get in~~	get off	hang out	pick up
take off	turn back	turn out	turn up	

a Our plane ....*got in*........[1] at 8 p.m. yesterday evening and our friends .... us ....[2] from the airport. Today, we're setting off for the islands.

b We ....[3] to a good start this morning and managed to cycle about 20 km, but then we had to ....[4] because of the rain.

c The tour bus didn't ....[5] so we decided to go on a walking tour instead. Later, we found out that the bus had ....[6].

d Our departure was delayed and the plane ....[7] two hours late, but it ....[8] OK because we made friends with some other travellers and ....[9] with them in the airport café.

2 Find two other phrasal verbs in the blog entries.

....

3 Which blog entry describes a day that:

- started well but ended badly ....
- started badly and ended well ....
- was good and nothing bad happened. ....

Challenge ⭐

4 Describe a trip that started badly but ended well. Write a paragraph in your notebook. Use multi-word verbs from this lesson.

› Multi-word verbs

Use of English

Mina: We're going away on holiday tomorrow. Can you look after our cat for a few days?

Sofia: Yes, of course! Where are you going?

Mina: We're going to Paris. I'm really looking forward to it! My uncle is putting us up in his flat. We wanted to go last year, but we never got round to it.

Sofia: That sounds nice. What are you planning to do?

Mina: We're going to look round the museums and eat out a lot! We're coming back on Tuesday.

Check!
Complete the rules with words from the box. There is one extra word.

object	pronoun	subject	three	two

Some multi-word verbs have ....[1] words. For example *get up*, *sit down*.

Some multi-word verbs have ....[2] words. For example *get away with*, *put up with*.

Some multi-word verbs do not have an ....[3]. For example *grow up*, *come apart*.

Two-word verbs with an object sometimes have to separate when the object is a ....[4].

Focus

1   Read the conversation above between Mina and Sofia. Underline the multi-word verbs. Match them with definitions.

   a   Two three-part verbs. *look forward to,* ....

   b   Three verbs that don't have an object. ....

   c   One verb that separates after an object which is a pronoun.

      ....

Practice

2 **Circle the correct option to complete the sentences.**

a Have you *heard from / heard* Grace since she went to Australia?

b We missed our flight and *ended up / ended* waiting nearly ten hours at the airport for the next one.

c It took us ages to *find out / find* the hotel because it was along a tiny lane with no road signs.

d The concert *ended up / ended* just after eight, but I hung out with my friends for a while afterwards.

e We went to the sports club during the day, but we *joined in / joined* our parents in the evenings.

f I went to the reception desk to *find out / find* about hiring bikes.

g I don't know the number of the restaurant, but we can *look it up / look it* online.

h A hotel minibus will *pick us up / pick us* from the airport.

⊙ Get it right!

Remember that the meaning of multi-word verbs is often different from their single-word equivalents.

- end (= finish): *The sightseeing tour **ended** at about 12.30, then we stopped for lunch.*

- end up (= be the final situation or place): *The weather was so bad, we **ended up** staying in our room all week.*

- find something (= locate something): *I can't **find** my keys.*

- find something out (= discover information): *Can you **find out** the name of the hotel?*

Challenge ★

3 **Rewrite the underlined part of each sentence using a multi-word verb.**

a What time are you <u>returning</u> home? .....*coming back*..... (come)

b We aren't eating at home tonight. We're going to <u>have dinner in a restaurant.</u> .... (eat)

c We were driving along a country road when the car suddenly <u>stopped working</u>. .... (break)

d I caught a cold last winter, but <u>I recovered from it</u> very quickly. .... (get)

e The wildfires were fierce and it took three days to <u>extinguish them</u>. .... (put)

f I don't understand this word. Can you <u>find its meaning</u> in the dictionary? .... (look)

〉 Past continuous passive

Use of English

Check!

Complete the rules.

We form the past continuous passive by using the ....[1] form of *be* (was or were) followed by the ....[2] participle of *be* (being) and the ....[3] participle of the verb.

subject	past of *be*	present participle of *be*	past participle of main verb
The castle	*was*	*being*	*renovated.*

We wanted to visit the castle, but it was closed for repairs. The roof was being mended. The windows were being painted. New drainpipes were being installed.

Focus

1 **Read the caption under the picture. Underline the past forms of *be*. Draw a wavy line under the present participles of *be*. Circle the main verb.**

2 **Complete the sentences using the past continuous passive of the verbs in brackets.**

   a She ....*was being interviewed*........ (interview) for a job yesterday.

   b The new teachers .... (introduce) to the parents this morning.

   c The visitors waited in the lounge while the food .... (prepare).

   d I suddenly realised that I .... (watch) .

   e The taxi broke down while she .... (drive) home.

   f We waited in the airport building while the plane .... (refuel).

Practice

3 **Are these sentences correct? Tick (✓) the correct sentences and correct the ones that contain errors on the line below.**

a   The dining room was being decorate for the party. ☐

The dining room was being decorated for the party.

b   Some people wasn't being invited to join the group. ☐

....

c   Coffee and tea wasn't being provided on our day trip. ☐

....

d   They weren't being told the real reason for the delay. ☐

....

e   We were being explained the history by the tour guide. ☐

....

f   What kind of food was been served for dinner? ☐

....

Challenge ★

4 **Complete the sentences with the past continuous passive of the verbs in the box.**

~~clean~~   explain   perform   decorate   repair   unload

a   We couldn't go to our hotel rooms because they ....*were being cleaned*...... .

b   They couldn't drive their car because it ....

c   Some treasures were found in the palace when it ....

d   They visited an amphitheatre where a play ....

e   We waited in the lobby while our suitcases ....

f   The visitors waited in the bus while the tour schedule

....

› 3.4 Responsible tourism

1 Complete the conversation with phrases from the box.

Is it a kind of treehouse?	No electricity then?	They're beautiful!
Where did you eat?	Did you bring back any souvenirs?	
Did you see any wildlife?	~~Yes, please!~~	

Shuli: Do you want to see some photos from our holiday in Thailand?

Victor: .Yes, please!.. [1]

Shuli: It was amazing! Look at this photo of our hotel!

Victor: .... [2]

Shuli: It's a kind of eco-hotel designed to have a low impact on the environment.

Victor: .... [3]

Shuli: The houses are owned by people in the village and they prepared all of our food. It was delicious and all locally sourced!

Victor: .... [4]

Shuli: We used solar energy for lighting and wood to make a fire.

Victor: .... [5]

Shuli: A local guide took us into the forest and we saw birds and monkeys. You have to keep to the trail and of course not leave any rubbish.

Victor: .... [6]

Shuli: Yes, we did. These wooden bowls were made by craft workers in the village.

Victor: .... [7]

2 Tick (✓) the words that describe Shuli's holiday. Put a cross (✗) next to the words that don't describe her holiday.

☐ eco-friendly accommodation   ☐ litter   ☐ buying local souvenirs

☐ air conditioning   ☐ helping local economy   ☐ wildlife products

☐ helping endangered species   ☐ eating local produce

☐ international hotel chain   ☐ saving precious resources

Challenge ★

3 What would you like / not like about Shuli's holiday? Write in your notebook.

> 3.5 A different type of family holiday

1 **Match the two parts of each word and write them next to the correct definition.**

a At risk of becoming extinct. ....*endangered*....

b Types of animals, birds or fish. ....

c Watching and observing something to check its safety. ....

d Protecting something from destruction. ....

e Keep safe from harm or injury. ....

f Continuing to live, despite problems. ....

g Not looking after something. ....

h When species live together. ....

~~endan~~	istence
conser	tect
spec	ies
coex	vation
mon	ival
pro	lect
neg	itor
surv	~~gered~~

2 **Complete the text with words from Exercise 1.**

Visit our wildlife sanctuary! We are working hard to .... *protect* .... ¹ wildlife. There are many .... ² species of birds and insects. We .... ³ their numbers and help to ensure their .... ⁴. So many forests and fields have been lost due to increased human population. The .... ⁵ of their natural habitat is also important. We also provide a home for animals that have been .... ⁶ or mistreated. Our goal is the peaceful .... ⁷ of humans and wildlife.

Challenge

3 **Complete the sentences using your own ideas.**

a We need to ensure the survival of endangered species because ....
....

b The conservation of rainforests is important because ....
....

> 3.6 Is tourism a good thing?

1   **Look at the photo and read the article. What is the best title for the article? Tick (✓) your answer.**

☐   Climbers enjoy camping on Mount Everest

☐   Crowds cause traffic jams on Mount Everest

☐   Volunteers pick up litter after climbing trips

Mount Everest is the highest mountain in the world, and a place that we think of as the loneliest place in the world, isolated and untouched. But the reality is quite different. Climbing Mount Everest is big business. Tour operators charge thousands of dollars to organise expeditions and take climbers up Everest's slopes, an industry which employs many local people from small hotel owners to mountain guides. Some of the revenue is used by the Nepalese government to pay for environmental conservation. Despite the expense, tour routes are getting more and more crowded every year, with climbers sometimes waiting over an hour to get to the top in long queues down the side of the mountain. But at what cost to the environment? Climbers not only erode the mountainside, they also leave kilograms of litter behind, which is expensive to clean up.

2   **Answer the questions.**

a   What is increasing every year? ....

b   Who makes money from the tours? ....

c   What do climbers pay money for? ....

d   Why do you think climbers leave a lot of litter? ....

3   **Think about the following statement. Write three reasons for and against the proposition in your notebook.**

> **'Tourists should be banned from protected natural areas.'**

Challenge ⭐

4   **What is your opinion on the statement? Write a short paragraph in your notebook.**

> Compound adjectives

Use of English

A five-day trip to
Istanbul

- Visit a 5000-year-old palace
- Stay in a comfortable well-run hotel
- Try locally produced food and drink
- Visit world-famous museums
- Buy handmade jewellery

A compound adjective combines two or more words to create one adjective. We can combine adjectives, adverbs or nouns.

Many compound adjectives combine a number with a noun or a measurement. For example, *a three-hour journey, a 16-wheel truck.*

Many compound nouns combine an adjective with a present or past participle. For example, *a life-changing experience, an open-minded approach.*

Most compound nouns use a hyphen when they appear before a noun, but not when they follow. *It is a well-run hotel. The hotel is well run.*

We don't use a hyphen with adverbs that end in *-ly*, for example *internationally known,* or with colours, for example *dark green.*

Some compound nouns are so common that they have become joined into one word. For example, *homemade.*

Check!

Read the trip advertisement above. Underline the compound adjectives and write them after the correct descriptions.

a   adverb + adjective ....*well-run*........

b   noun+ adjective ....

c   adverb with *-ly* + adjective ....

d   number + a noun ....

e   a compound adjective that has become one word ....

Focus

1 **Complete the compound adjectives with words from the box.**

aged	minute	green
minded	well	world

a   A five-....................... video

b   A ....-eyed cat

c   An open- .... person

d   A ....-made jacket

e   A middle-....................... man

f   A ....-class stadium

Practice

2   **Use the words in brackets to form an appropriate compound adjective to complete the sentences.**

a   We visited Montreal which is in the ...*French-speaking*... (French speak) part of Canada.

b   The square was decorated with .... (multi colour) flags.

c   The bed was too small even for an .... (average size) adult.

d   At the airport you can use the .... (self service) check-in desks.

e   The bedrooms have .... (old fashion) ceiling fans instead of air-conditioning.

f   Passengers who fly with .... (low cost) airlines expect to pay for food and drink on board.

Challenge

3   **Rewrite the underlined parts using compound nouns.**

a   The boy was <u>eight years old</u>. He was ...*an eight-year-old*.. boy.

b   The trip <u>took three days</u>. It was a .... trip.

c   The bread was <u>made at home</u>. It was .... bread.

d   The students <u>had a good education</u>. They were .... students.

e   The town <u>has a dense population</u>. It was a .... town.

f   Our teacher <u>has a kind heart</u>. Our teacher is a .... person.

〉 Participle adjectives

Use of English

We're going on a school ski trip. I'm so excited!

This ski trip is so exciting!

Check!
Complete the rules with words from the box.

~~adjective~~	causes	feel	past	present

We can use the present or past participle of a verb to make an ....*adjective*........[1].

The......................[2] participle, or -*ed* form, usually describes how you......................[3] in response to something. We don't use this form to describe things.

The......................[4] participle, or -*ing* form, usually describes the thing that......................[5] the feeling.

Focus

1 Circle the participle adjectives in these sentences.

a Travelling by train is so (boring.)

b The boys were tired of playing their game.

c The film had a thrilling ending.

d We were surprised by a man who was following us.

e They were walking uphill and all of them were exhausted.

f It was an amazing trip that will not be forgotten.

Practice

2 Complete the sentences using the correct form of the word in brackets.

a The museum wants to find ways to make people more ......*interested*...... (interest) in history.

b Both locals and tourists are getting really .... (excite) about the festival at the weekend.

c Waiting around at airports can be really .... (bore), so remember to take a good book.

d The walk to the top of the hill was pretty .... (tire), but the view from the top was .... (amaze).

e I think a trip is more .... (excite) if you haven't been to the country before and don't know what to expect.

3 Are these sentences correct? Focus on the <u>underlined</u> words. Put a tick (✓) by the correct sentences. Make changes to the incorrect ones.

a Could you send me some more <u>detail</u>^{ed} information about prices and dates? ☐

b When we arrived in the village, the only café was <u>close</u>, so we just got some drinks from a small shop that was <u>opened</u>. ☐

c The staff at the hotel were really <u>welcoming</u> and gave us lots of tips about where to go. ☐

d Some people get quite <u>stressful</u> about travelling. ☐

e We were a bit <u>concern</u> about communicating, but everyone spoke really good English. ☐

f The building was really <u>impressing</u> – I took loads of photos. ☐

g By the end of the week, I felt totally <u>relax</u> and didn't want to come home! ☐

h It was a really long journey and we were all really <u>pleased</u> when we finally arrived. ☐

Challenge ⭐

4 Complete the sentences with participle adjective forms of verbs from the box.

| amuse | annoy | disappoint | ~~excite~~ | fascinate | tire |

a The trip was the most ....*exciting*........ tour I have ever done.

b We were really .... at the end of the day and went to bed early.

c Some guests felt .... about the noise of music late at night.

d The tour guide's explanations were .... and often made us laugh.

e We spent several hours in the Grand Palace. It was the most .... part of the tour.

f We were .... by the weather as it rained most of the time.

> 3.7 Improve your writing

1 Read the travel review. Tick (✓) the things that it mentions.

☐ Food   ☐ Hotel   ☐ Transport

☐ Guide   ☐ Sightseeing   ☐ Weather

Trip review: **Five-day tour to Machu Picchu**

This trip was amazing! I learned so much and saw so many incredible sights.

The first day, we stayed in Cuzco. There was a great street market and we hiked up to a castle built by the Incas centuries ago that overlooked the valley. The second day, we went hiking in the Sacred Valley. We saw plenty of wildlife, including some llamas. We stopped for a rest and a swim at a hot spring! The third day, we headed off for Machu Picchu. The hike up the mountain was quite challenging, but the views were breathtaking! This was my favourite part of the tour. Our guide, Salvador, told us so much about the history of the Incas.

The hotels we stayed at were all family-run and the owners and staff were incredibly kind. Some of the food was a little unusual for me, for example the ceviche, but all of the vegetarian dishes were delicious!

We bought locally made souvenirs, including some handmade pottery. The only problem? It was too short! I could have stayed on for at least three more days. I highly recommend this tour!

2 In the trip review, circle the positive adjectives and underline the negative adjectives.

3 Find a word for each of the following.

     a A type of food. ....   **d** A type of building. ....

     b A type of animal. ....   **e** A type of craft. ....

     c A feature of landscape. ....

4 Choose a place that you have visited on holiday. Make notes in your notebook under the headings from Exercise 1. Include some positive and some negative points. Then write a trip review.

> 3.8 Fiction

1   Read the first paragraph of the chapter from *The Summer Book* by Tove Jansson again. Then read the questions and circle the correct answers.

The Morning Swim

IT WAS AN EARLY, VERY WARM MORNING IN JULY, and it had rained during the night. The bare granite steamed, the moss and crevices were drenched with moisture, and all the colours everywhere had deepened. Below the veranda, the vegetation in the morning shade was like a rainforest of lush, evil leaves and flowers, which she had to be careful not to break as she searched. She held one hand in front of her mouth and was constantly afraid of losing her balance.

"What are you doing?" asked little Sophia.

"Nothing," her grandmother answered. "That is to say," she added angrily, "I'm looking for my false teeth."

a   Which of these are described in the first paragraph of the story?

colours	light and dark	natural features	plants	sensations
smells	sounds	time of day	weather	

b   How would you describe the vegetation near the house?

A thick   B dry   C tidy

c   How does the grandmother feel about walking through the vegetation?

A confident   B excited   C nervous

d   Why was the grandmother holding her hand in front of her mouth?

A   She was afraid.

B   She was embarrassed.

C   She was sleepy.

e   Why do you think the grandmother first says 'Nothing' and then changes her mind?

A   She needs some help to find her teeth.

B   She wants to be honest with the little girl.

C   She doesn't care what the little girl thinks.

2   Imagine that you are the little girl, Sophia. In your notebook, write a short description of your first day staying with your grandmother on the island.

4 ▶ Science

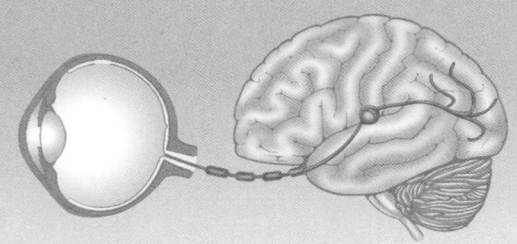

› 4.1 The science of colour

1   **Complete the text with words from this lesson.**

| cones | light | ~~retina~~ | shades of colour |

The human eye is lined with a light-sensitive tissue called the

...........*retina*.........¹ that sends signals to the brain. It

contains two types of receptors: rods and ....².

The rods perceive white, grey and black. The cones can

perceive colours, but only when there is enough

.........................³. That's why we can't see colours

at night-time. There are three types of cones that respond

to short, medium and long wavelengths. Different colours

have different wavelengths. People have different levels of

sensitivity to different wavelengths and that is why

.........................⁴ may be perceived differently by

each person.

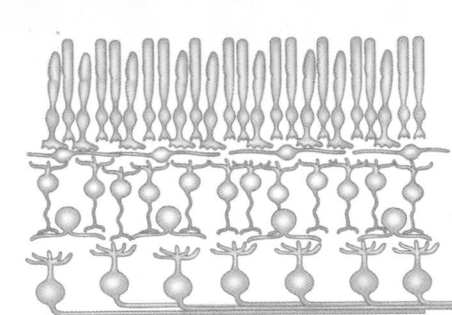

2   **Match the headings in the box with the sentences.**

1 A few people are tetrachromatic.	**3** Most humans are trichromatic.
2 Birds are tetrachromatic.	**4** Some people are colour-blind.

a   [   ]   They have three different colour receptors and can detect red, blue and green.

b   [   ]   They have only two colour receptors. Their eyes only detect blue and green.

c   [   ]   They can detect far more different shades of colour than other people because they have four colour receptors.

d   [   ]   This helps them find food.

Language tip

The prefix *tri-* comes from a Greek word meaning 'three'.

The prefix *tetra-* comes from a Greek word meaning 'four'.

> 4.2 Deadly diseases

1 **Complete the crossword.**

Across

1 The Black Death was an example of this type of disease. (6)

3 An injection that protects you from disease. (11)

7 A period of isolation from others in case you have a disease. (10)

8 Edward Jenner discovered an inoculation for this disease. (8)

Down

2 Drugs, like streptomycin, that treat bacterial infections. (11)

4 Like typhoid, it is caused by contaminated water. (7)

5 An illness that affects people in many countries, for example COVID-19. (8)

6 Keeping water supplies clean and healthy. (10)

9 A worldwide pandemic that started in 2019. (5, 2)

10 In the 1950s, it was found that streptomycin cures this disease. (12)

2 **Circle the clue numbers for words that are illnesses. Draw a square round the clue numbers for words that describe prevention or treatment.**

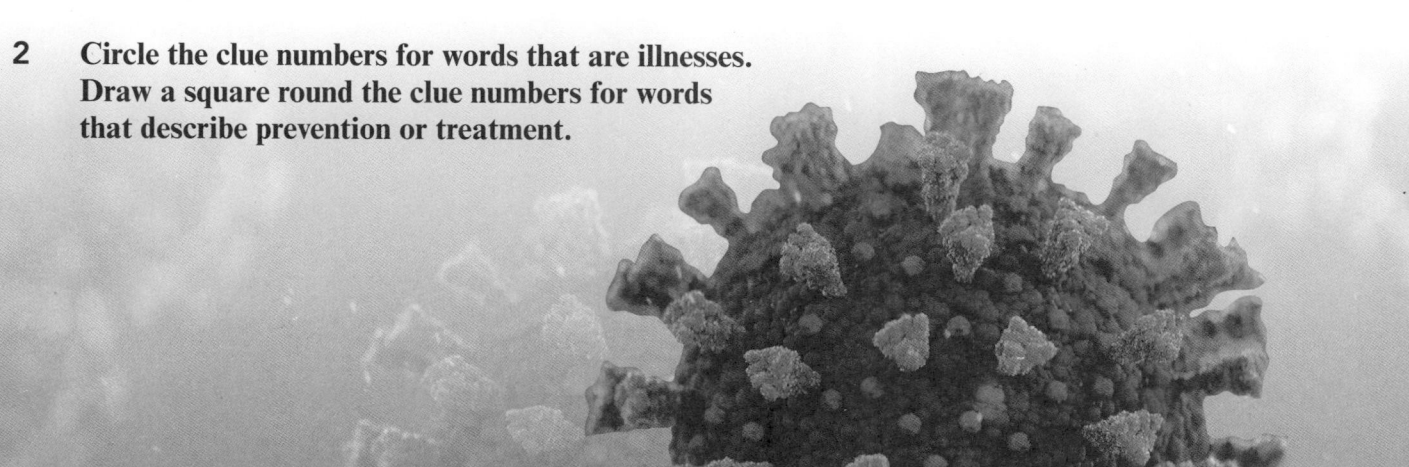

> 4.3 What makes us the same? What makes us different?

1 Read the information. Then complete the quiz by circling the correct answers.

A **genome** is a complete set of DNA* for an organism, including all the genes (segments of DNA that code for specific traits). In humans, a copy of the entire genome is contained in all cells that have a nucleus. Genes contain information that is responsible for physical characteristics. Most genes are the same in all people, but a small number of genes (about 0.5 per cent) are slightly different.

*deoxyribonucleic acid

The Human Genome Project
(HGP) was an international research programme with the goal of identifying the complete sequence of all human genes. The HGP gave scientists the ability, for the first time, to read nature's complete genetic blueprint for a human being. This could help scientists to identify genetic diseases and also develop new treatments for them.

1 Genetics is the study of
   A how characteristics are inherited.
   B how to identify each person.

2 Your genetic information or genome is stored in
   A some parts of your brain.
   B almost every cell of your body.

3 Your genome is
   A all of your DNA.
   B your unique genes.

4 Everyone's genome is
   A very similar.
   B completely different.

5 A single gene can be responsible for
   A your favourite colour.
   B your hair colour.

6 The main goal of the Human Genome Project was to
   A identify each person's fingerprints.
   B determine the sequence of human DNA.

7 Thanks to the HGP, scientists can
   A understand genetic processes.
   B identify genetic diseases.

8 Future uses of the HGP could be to
   A develop new energy sources.
   B develop new medical treatments.

Challenge

2 Think of two people in your family who are similar. In your notebook, write about their similarities and differences.

› Conjunctions

Check!

1 Read the caption. Underline the conjunctions and the *-ing* forms.

2 Complete the rules with the correct words from the box.

> after ~~conjunctions~~ comma
> first *-ing* form same

We can use ....*conjunctions*..........[1] to join two clauses.

Conjunctions are words such as *when*, *while* and ....[2].

A conjunction can be followed by the ....[3] of a verb.

The clause with the conjunction can be ....[4] or second. If it is first, the clause is followed by a ....[5].

When using an *-ing* form, make sure that the subject of both clauses is the ....[6].

Always wear safety goggles when pouring the solutions into the flask.

Watch carefully while adding each solution to the mixture.

After mixing these three solutions, you will see a change in colour.

Focus

1 **Complete the sentences using the conjunction and *-ing* form of the verb in brackets.**

a ...*Before starting*... (Before; start) the experiment, you should wash your hands.

b He read a book .... (while; wait) for the bus.

c .... (After; learn) about the effects of colour, I decided to paint my room.

d .... (When; cycle) to school, he always wears a helmet.

e They wrote a report .... (after; finish) the experiment.

f Did you talk to anyone .... (while; work) in the library?

Practice

2 **Are these sentences correct? Tick (✓) the correct sentences and correct the ones that contain errors on the line below.**

a After studied the picture for 10 seconds, people were asked to describe the main colours.

After studying the picture for 10 seconds, people were asked to describe the ......

main colours. ....

b It's important to think about colour when design a poster. ☐

....

c While paint a picture, it's important to be aware of how the light changes the colours you see. ☐

....

d After watched the video, I understand a bit more about how we see colour. ☐

....

e According to research, when cycling during the day, you're most visible in bright yellow clothes. ☐

....

Challenge ⭐

3 **Write sentences using a conjunction followed by the *-ing* form of the verb in brackets. Remember to add a comma if necessary.**

a he was climbing / he fell and broke his leg (when)

When climbing, he fell and broke his leg. ....

b went to China / she completed her degree (after)

....

c they started their project / they did lots of research (before)

....

d her eyes were tested / she got a prescription for new glasses (after)

....

e we listened to music / we were travelling on the train (while)

....

› Present and past simple passive

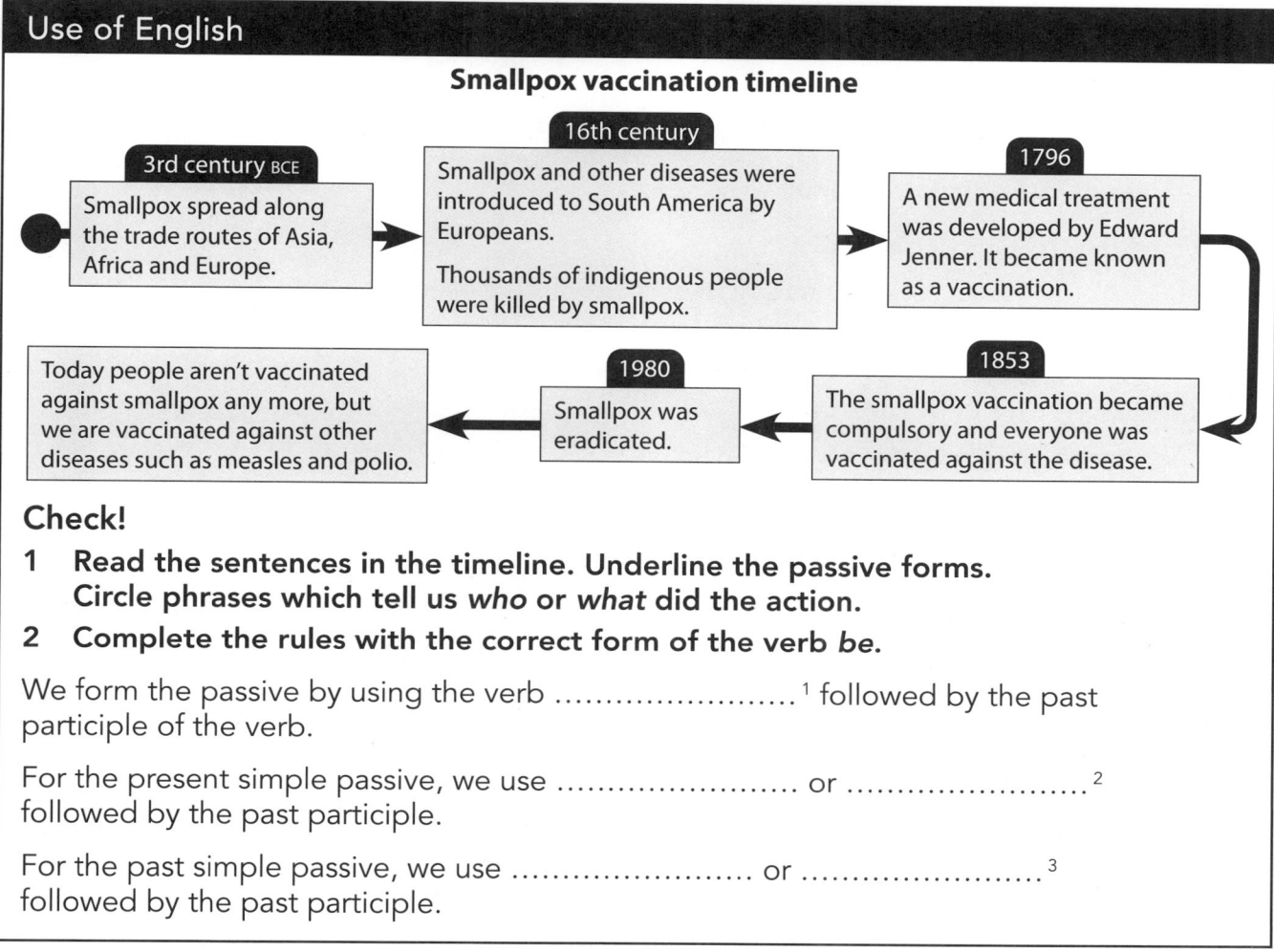

Smallpox vaccination timeline

3rd century BCE
Smallpox spread along the trade routes of Asia, Africa and Europe.

16th century
Smallpox and other diseases were introduced to South America by Europeans.
Thousands of indigenous people were killed by smallpox.

1796
A new medical treatment was developed by Edward Jenner. It became known as a vaccination.

1853
The smallpox vaccination became compulsory and everyone was vaccinated against the disease.

1980
Smallpox was eradicated.

Today people aren't vaccinated against smallpox any more, but we are vaccinated against other diseases such as measles and polio.

Check!

1 **Read the sentences in the timeline. Underline the passive forms. Circle phrases which tell us *who* or *what* did the action.**

2 **Complete the rules with the correct form of the verb *be*.**

We form the passive by using the verb ....¹ followed by the past participle of the verb.

For the present simple passive, we use .... or ....² followed by the past participle.

For the past simple passive, we use .... or ....³ followed by the past participle.

Focus

1 **Use the information in the timeline to answer the questions. Use complete sentences. If you are not sure, use *probably*.**

   a Who spread smallpox along the trade routes?

   It was probably spread by travellers and traders.... .

   b Who introduced smallpox to South America?

   It ....

   c What killed the indigenous people?

   They ....

   d Who developed a vaccine for smallpox?

   It ....

2 **Complete the sentences using the present or past simple passive.**

a Vaccines ......*were used*...... (use) by the ancient Chinese 2000 years ago.

b The results of Jenner's experiment .... (publish) in a scientific journal in 1798.

c Nowadays, most older people .... (vaccinate) against flu every year.

d Edward Jenner .... (know) as the person who discovered the smallpox vaccination.

e In 2020, millions of people .... (kill) by a virus known as COVID-19.

f Lots of research .... (need) to develop vaccines.

Practice

3 **Complete the sentences using a relative pronoun (*who, which*) and a passive form of the verb in brackets. You may need a present simple passive or a past simple passive.**

a The research involved 40,000 volunteers ...*who were given*... (give) the new vaccine.

b Graphene, ... (discover) in 2004, is the thinnest known substance.

c Chlorophyll is a green substance .... (find) in all plants.

d Our sense of balance is controlled by tiny organs .... (locate) in the ear.

e A honeycomb is made up of hexagons .... (arrange) together in a familiar pattern.

> ### ⊙ Get it right!
>
> Remember that we often use a passive verb form in a relative clause to give more details about a person or thing.
>
> *Doctors still use penicillin, **which was discovered** in the early 20th century.* ✔
>
> *Doctors still use penicillin, which discovered in the early 20th century.* ✗
>
> *We learned about Tu Youyou, **who was awarded** a Nobel Prize for developing treatments for malaria.*

Challenge

4 **Write questions using the present or past passive in your notebook. Then try to answer them. Look online to help you.**

a When / X-rays / invent .....*When were X-rays invented?*....

b How / people / kill / the Black Death?

c What types of illness / not treated / antibiotics / today

d How / bacterial infections / treat / nowadays

> 4.4 Live and let live

1 **Circle the correct answers.**

    a Which of these animals is a type of cattle?

        A sheep   **B** (cows)   **C** leopards

    b Which of these animals is a predator?

        A lion   **B** giraffe   **C** zebra

    c Which of these animals is in danger of extinction?

        A cow   **B** cheetah   **C** goat

    d Which of these is not an example of a crop?

        A cotton   **B** rice   **C** goats

    e Which of these is an example of wildlife?

        A trees   **B** plants   **C** birds

    f Which of these is a type of livestock?

        A sheep   **B** elephants   **C** lions

2 **Write the name of each animal. Circle the names of wild animals.**
Underline the names of livestock animals.

b ....

c ....

d ....

a ...(lion)..............

e ....

f ....

g ....

Challenge

3 **What are the top ten most endangered animals in the world? Go online to research and find the answer. Then write it in your notebook.**

> 4.5 The circle of life

1 **Read the texts. What do these stories have in common?**

A Sea turtles were once hunted for their meat and shells, but are now a protected species. They face danger from large boats as well as plastic in the ocean. As more beaches are being taken over by tourism in Thailand, turtles are losing their nesting sites and are vulnerable to extinction. Conservation volunteers collect the eggs and take them to a conservation centre. After the eggs have hatched, the baby turtles are taken to the sea. Baby turtles can be prey to larger fish and sharks, but adult turtles have few predators and can live up to 60 years.

B The human population in China has been increasing. As a result, giant pandas have been losing the bamboo forest that is their natural habitat and provides them with food. To solve this problem, the Chinese government has created dozens of protected areas where pandas can live safely. Today there are 1800 giant pandas in the wild, up from 1100 in 1980. These reserves have also protected other small mammals and birds that together create an interdependent ecosystem.

C In 1930, there were over 10 million elephants in Africa. Today there are just 400,000. Elephants are herbivores and are part of a fragile ecosystem where birds, insects and other pollinators all play an important role. Their only predators are humans. They are hunted and killed by poachers for their ivory tusks. This has greatly reduced their numbers and they are now in danger of becoming extinct. Today, there are several wildlife sanctuaries in Africa rescuing orphaned and wounded elephants before returning them to the wild.

2 **For each question, write the correct letter A, B or C from Exercise 1.**

Which animals:

a have increased their numbers? [ ]

b have been losing their access to food? [ ]

c are held in captivity for a while? [ ]

d have been losing access to their habitat? [ ]

e can get killed by pollution? [ ]

f are killed, but not for food? [ ]

g used to be killed by humans for food? [ ]

> 4.6 Views on zoos

1 **Read the opinions. Complete the text with missing prepositions.**

Do you agree .... [1] wildlife safari holidays?

A I think they're a good way to earn money to help protect animals .... [2] poachers and other dangers. Some of them succeed .... [3] breeding animals, which helps to save the animals .... [4] extinction, as well as ensuring genetic diversity.

B I think that people driving around in cars and trucks and chasing animals to get photos is frightening for the animals. Some of the animals can respond .... [5] humans in a hostile and aggressive way, so it can be dangerous too. It's also destructive to the environment.

C I don't believe .... [6] zoos or keeping animals in enclosures and cages where I think animals lose their natural instincts, so compared .... [7] zoos, I think safari holidays are the best way to see animals in their natural habitat.

D I'm in favour .... [8] wildlife sanctuaries where they take care of orphaned and sick animals and then release them into the wild. If you can see animals there, you don't need to go to a safari park.

E I don't approve .... [9] travelling thousands of miles by plane to go on a safari. Just think of the carbon footprint! You can see animals much better on TV and video nowadays.

2 **Which of the opinions are for wildlife safaris and which are against?**

....

Challenge

3 **In your notebook, write your opinion of safari holidays, wildlife parks or zoos. Start like this:**

I agree / don't agree with safari holidays because ...

I approve / don't approve of wildlife parks because ...

I'm / I'm not in favour of zoos because ...

› Present perfect continuous

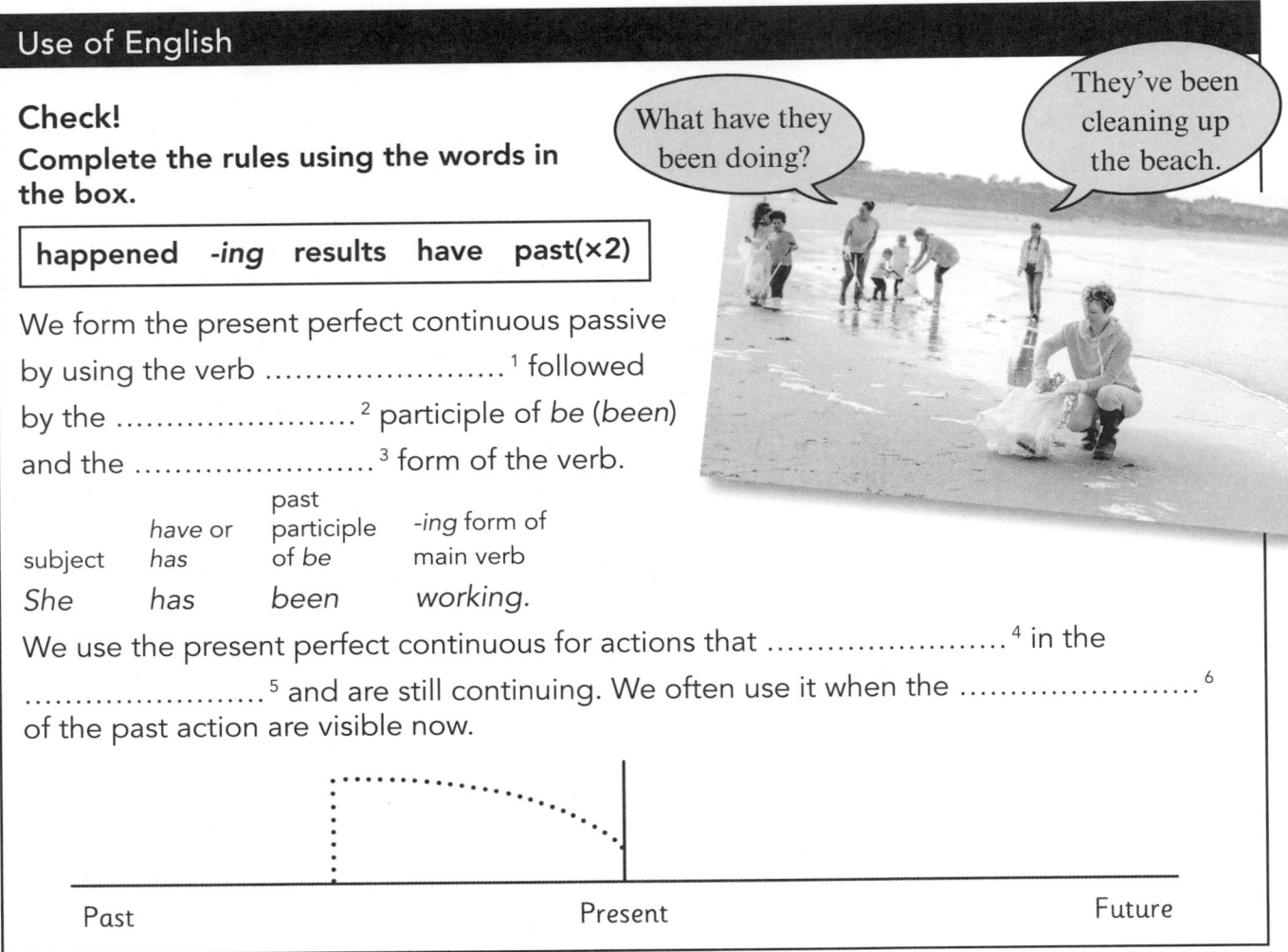

Use of English

Check!
Complete the rules using the words in the box.

happened   -ing   results   have   past(×2)

What have they been doing?

They've been cleaning up the beach.

We form the present perfect continuous passive

by using the verb .... ¹ followed

by the .... ² participle of *be* (*been*)

and the .... ³ form of the verb.

subject	*have* or *has*	past participle of *be*	*-ing* form of main verb
She	*has*	*been*	*working.*

We use the present perfect continuous for actions that .... ⁴ in the

.... ⁵ and are still continuing. We often use it when the .... ⁶

of the past action are visible now.

Past   Present   Future

Focus

1   **Look at the photo and the dialogue. Underline the present perfect continuous forms.**

2   **Complete the sentences using the present perfect continuous of the verb in brackets.**

a   They .*have been playing*. (play) a video game for two hours.

b   Vicky .... (study) Spanish for three years.

c   How long .... you .... (talk) on the phone?

d   We .... (not wait) here for very long.

e   His car is very dirty. Where .... he .... (drive)?

f   I .... (walk) for three hours and I'm very tired.

Practice

3 **Choose the correct verb form to complete the sentences. Look carefully at the underlined time phrases to help you.**

a In our science class, *we've been measuring / we are measuring* local air pollution levels <u>since the start of the year</u>.

b <u>In recent years</u>, lots of people *have been complaining / were complaining* about air quality.

c <u>Last term</u>, *we've been studying / we were studying* how plants get energy from sunlight.

d <u>Over the past three weeks</u>, *we've been watching / we were watching* a series of videos about how viruses work.

e <u>In our last lesson</u>, the teacher *has been carrying out / carried out* an experiment using liquid nitrogen.

f *I've been revising / I'm revising* <u>for ages</u>, but I still can't remember all of the chemical symbols.

 Get it right!

Remember that we often use a present perfect continuous form with a time phrase that refers to a period that started in the past and continues until now: *for a long time, since last year, recently.*

We've been planning this trip *for a long time.*

The students <u>have been raising</u> money for the project **since last summer.**

Recently, more students <u>have been cycling</u> to school.

Challenge

4 **Write sentences to explain what these people have been doing. Use the present perfect continuous of the phrases in the box.**

buy food for a party	have a shower	cook dinner
~~play football in the rain~~	repair your bike	walk in the snow

a Their clothes are covered in mud. ....*They've been playing football in the rain.*............

b Her hair is wet. ....

c Their kitchen smells of roast chicken. ....

d They are carrying shopping bags full of crisps and soft drinks. ....
....

e Our hats and coats are covered in snow. ....
....

f Your hands are covered in oil. ....
....

> Present perfect active and passive

Use of English

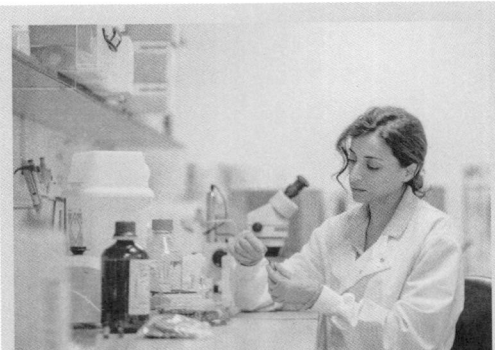

A new blood test has been developed that can detect early signs of cancer. Data have been collected from thousands of volunteers in a new research study. The results have shown a significant increase in early detection rates. Early detection has been found to be the key to successful treatment and cure.

Check!

1 **Read the caption. Underline the passive forms.**

2 **Choose the correct words.**

> We use the present perfect for events that happened in the *past / present*[1]. The event *is finished / continues up to now*[2] or *has / doesn't have*[3] a result that we can see now. We *use / don't use*[4] the present perfect for events that happened at a specific time in the past.

The present perfect active form uses *have* or *has* plus the past participle.

We *have raised* money for medical research.

The present perfect passive form uses *have* or *has* plus *been* plus the past participle.

Money *has been raised* for medical research.

Focus

1 **Complete the sentences using the verbs in brackets.**

a Many lives ..*have been saved*.. (save) by the new vaccine.

b This vaccine .... (test) on animals, but not on humans.

c Hundreds of volunteers .... (give) the new therapy.

d A single cure for all cancers .... (find) yet.

e New medical treatments .... (develop) using DNA.

f Why .... the research results .... (not publish) yet?

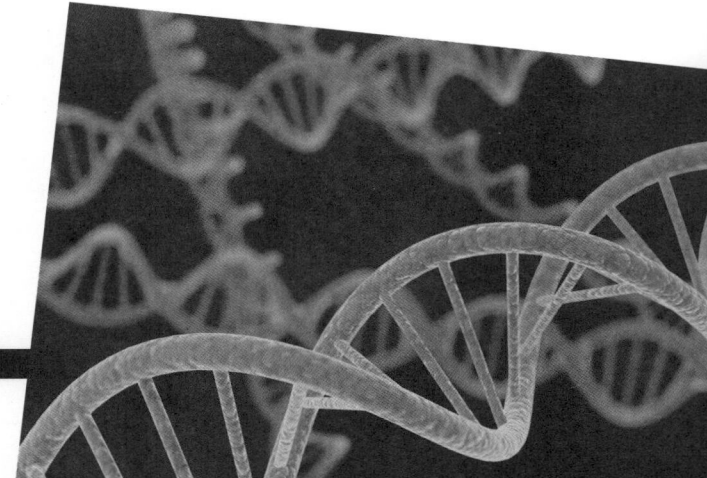

Practice

> **⊙ Get it right!**
>
> Remember to use the correct form *has* (singular) or *have* (plural) to go with the subject of a present perfect passive.
>
> *Several different <u>drugs</u> **have been developed** to treat the disease.*
>
> Use a singular verb form (*has*) after a countable noun.
>
> <u>Research</u> **has been carried out** into the causes of the condition. ✓
>
> *Researches have been carried out into the causes of the condition.* ✗

2 **Match the sentence halves. Think about meaning and grammar.**

a	In recent years, more evidence	**1**	have been influenced more and more by technology.
b	In the last couple of decades, our lives	**2**	has been damaged by human activities.
c	The winners of the prize	**3**	has been found about the link between exercise and mental health.
d	Sadly, a large area of the rainforest	**4**	have been recorded in the database.
e	Using an online survey, information	**5**	has been collected from more than 10,000 participants.
f	So far, the details of around a hundred patients	**6**	have already been informed via email.

Challenge

3 **Complete the paragraph with the present perfect active or passive.**

Robots …*have been used*…[1] (use) in hospitals for several years. A special robot …………………[2] (design) to find its way around the hospital to deliver medicines or to clean rooms. Some tasks, such as measuring a patient's vital signs, …………………[3] (take) over by robotic nurses. Recently, robots …………………[4] (become) more specialised. Some complex operations, such as knee replacements, …………………[5] (carry out) by surgical robots. Another kind of robot …………………[6] (train) to analyse data. Human doctors …………………[7] (not replace) by robots yet, but there's no doubt that robots …………………[8] (change) the way we think about medical care.

〉 4.7 Improve your writing

1 **What is your view on keeping pets at home?**
Complete the sentence with a reason for your opinion.

I think / don't think keeping a pet is a good idea

because ....……

2 **Read the arguments from an essay about keeping pets.**
Tick (✓) the arguments for, put a cross (✗) next to those against.

Is it right to keep pets?

☐ Children can learn about animals and how to look after them responsibly.

☐ Living in a person's home is nothing like their natural habitat.

☐ Pet animals can give affection and companionship to humans.

☐ Pets are usually looked after well and can live a long and healthy life.

☐ Some animals are bred to be pets and enjoy the company of humans.

☐ Some owners neglect their pets and don't give them enough exercise.

☐ Some pets can be dangerous to their owners or to others.

☐ Vet bills and health insurance for pets can be expensive.

3 **Which sentences could be from the introduction (write 'I')?**
Which sentences could be from the conclusion (write 'C')?

.... Many people keep pets at home and enjoy looking after them.

.... People should only have pets if they can look after them properly.

.... Wild animals shouldn't be kept as pets.

.... People have kept animals as pets since ancient times.

4 **Use the notes in Exercise 2 to write an essay to answer**
the question: *What is your view on keeping pets at home?*
Add your own ideas. Use connectives to link your ideas.

For example: *In the first place, pet animals can give affection and companionship to humans.*

Writing tip
Connectives
First, To start, In the first place
Second, In addition, Furthermore
Third, Finally
For example, such as, like, therefore, for this reason, because
However, but, although, while … whereas,
not only … but also …
In conclusion, To conclude, To sum up

> 4.8 Poetry

This poem was written in 1851 by a famous English poet. His poetry was often inspired by myths and legends, by human relationships, and also by nature.

1 **Read the poem and try to visualise the scene in your mind's eye.**

The Eagle

He clasps the crag with crooked hands;

Close to the sun in lonely lands,

Ring'd with the azure world, he stands.

The wrinkled sea beneath him crawls;

He watches from his mountain walls,

And like a thunderbolt he falls.

Alfred, Lord Tennyson

clasps: grips, holds tightly
crag: cliff or rock
crooked: not straight
azure: bright blue
ring'd: surrounded

2 **Read the poem again. Answer the questions in your notebook.**

a Write three adjectives to describe the eagle in this poem.

b Where is the eagle?

c What are the 'crooked hands'?

d Why does he 'fall' at the end of the poem?

e Which words rhyme in the poem?

f Summarise the story of the poem in one or two sentences.

g What does the writer want us to feel about the eagle?

Challenge

3 **Choose an animal that you like. Write a short poem in your notebook describing it in a way that will make the reader admire its beauty.**

5 ▶ Technology

> 5.1 Social media and you

1 Complete the questions with words from the box.

| emojis hashtag ~~likes~~ meme platform |
| posts selfies spam tweet vlog |

a Do you think people worry too much about how many ......*likes*........ they get for their ....?

b How do you feel if other people on your social media .... seem to be having more fun than you?

c What do you do to stop getting lots of .... on your social media feed?

d Do you prefer to connect with friends by sending a .... or by sharing photos?

e Do your friends post .... of themselves in new clothes? How often do they post them?

f Have you ever posted a photo which became a popular ....?

g Do you use .... in the captions of photos you post on social media?

h What kind of feelings do you often express using ....?

i Which do you think is better, writing a blog or posting a .... on YouTube?

2 In your notebook, answer the questions with information about yourself.

Challenge ⭐

3 In your notebook, write about three things you like and three things you dislike about using social media.

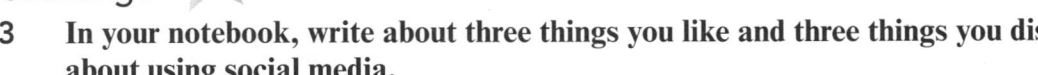

> 5.2 The home of the future

1 **Read the text. For each gap, circle the correct word from 1–10 below.**

Social robots

Technology is transforming our lives. It's changing the .... [1] we live, study and work. Smart technology means that devices .... [2] our homes, schools and workplaces will be .... [3] with each other as part of the Internet of Things. Robotics is a field .... [4] has made great advances in the development of social robots. Using artificial ...., [5] robots will be .... [6] to do many of the jobs that people do today. For example, robots will .... [7] care of elderly people at home. They will have sensors that .... [8] scan them for signs of hunger, thirst or illness. Has your digital assistant .... [9] you that you have a doctor's appointment for a check-up? A robot will measure your temperature and blood pressure and scan your health data for the last year. If you need medicine, a drone will .... [10] the prescription straight to your home within an hour.

1   path   (way)   how   road

2   in   of   over   with

3   transmitted   cooperated   contributed   connected

4   that   where   what   it

5   learning   brains   intelligence   skills

6   able   can   have   active

7   make   give   do   take

8   basically   mainly   certainly   automatically

9   said   called   asked   told

10   deliver   transmit   arrive   arrange

Challenge

2 **What do you think social robots will do in the future? What would you like them to do? Write three ideas in your notebook. Start like this:**

Social robots will help us to …

We'll have social robots at school for …

Social robots in restaurants and coffee shops will …

> 5.3 Digital media: good or bad?

1 **Read the sentences. Choose the best word.**

a   Social media is a way for people to (*interact*) / *concentrate* with each other.

b   Some people can get *addicted* / *engaged* to checking their phones for messages.

c   There is some *evidence* / *empathy* to show that online study tools can be very motivating.

d   Emails and messages can *interact* / *distract* you from your schoolwork.

e   You can enjoy *socialising* / *concentrating* with friends wherever you are.

f   You might feel less *empathy* / *addiction* for other people if you don't meet them in person.

g   It's easy to feel *addicted* / *left out* if you don't have the same social media platforms as your friends.

h   You can stay *connected* / *distracted* with all your friends at the same time.

2 **Read the sentences again. Which ones are positive, which are neutral and which are negative? Write the letters in the table.**

Positive	Neutral	Negative
	a	

3 **Write two more reasons for and against using social media.**

....

....

....

....

⟩ Relative clauses

Check!

1 Underline the relative clauses in the caption. Circle the information that each clause refers to.

2 Which clauses in the caption correspond to these rules?

   a To give extra, non-essential information. ....

   b To give essential, defining information. ....

   c To refer to the whole of a clause. ....

   In the rules above, when can *which* be replaced by *that*?

This is the latest version of a robot which is being developed as a companion for humans. The eyes, which are cameras, can recognise human faces and gestures. This robot can respond to human emotions, which you might find surprising.

Focus

1 **Match the two parts of each sentence. Say what each clause refers to.**

   a My proposal was accepted by the school committee ...4 (whole clause)...

   b The drones are used to investigate forest fires, ...

   c The new refrigerator has sensors ....

   d We learned to design robots ....

   e This is the digital teaching assistant ....

   f My computer crashed and couldn't be repaired ....

   1 which are quite frequent in this region.

   2 which can tell you when you have run out of food.

   3 which helps us during lessons.

   4 which made us really proud.

   5 which was quite upsetting.

   6 which was really exciting.

Practice

2 **Circle the correct word to complete the sentences. If two options are possible, circle both.**

a There's a link in the email **(which)** / what / **(that)** you can click on to go to the website.

b The website has lots of adverts, *which / what / that* is really annoying.

c My phone has an app *which / what / that* measures how many steps I do in a day.

d There's an app, *which / what / that* you can download for free, *which / what / that* shows you where you can refill your water bottle, *which / what / that* I think is really cool.

3 **Choose the correct verb form to complete the sentences.**

a You can add a hashtag which **help /** **(helps)** other people find the posts they want to read.

b He uses an app which **read / reads** the text on screen aloud.

c We keep in touch with family via social media, which **is / are** great.

d I've seen several laptops that all **look / looks** really good, which **make / makes** it hard to choose one.

> **⊘ Get it right!**
>
> Remember that we can use *which* or *that* in defining relative clauses.
>
> *Some people choose to have a profile picture* **which / that** *doesn't show their face.*
>
> We do not use *that* in non-defining relative clauses.
>
> *Some kids don't have a laptop at home,* **which** *means they can't do online homework.* ✓
>
> *Some kids don't have a laptop at home,* **that** *means they can't do online homework.* ✗

Challenge

4 **Complete the sentences with *which* and a phrase from the box.**

is quite a lot	is the end of next week	is held every year
was really nice	was quite complicated	~~you've been working on~~

A: Is this the science project *which you've been working on* ¹?

B: Yes, it is. I've entered it for the competition .... ² by the

Science Museum. I had to send in an application form, ... ³.
And 20 euros.

A: .... ⁴ really!

B: Yes, but my dad gave me the money, ... ⁵ of him.

A: When will you hear if you've been selected?

B: At the end of March.

A: .... ⁶ !

› Expressing the future

Use of English

Your schedule for tomorrow

A car will pick you up at 8 a.m. ......*b*.....

You will arrive at the airport at 9 a.m. ....

The plane leaves at 10.15 a.m. ....

The plane arrives at 11.45 a.m. ....

A representative will meet you at the airport. ....

You will be taken to your hotel by car. ....

You are going to do a tour of the city. ....

The team are meeting you for lunch at 12.30 p.m. ....

Check!
Read the schedule. Find examples of the following.

a   Future passive with *will*.

b   *Will* for information about the future.

c   Present continuous for personal arrangements.

d   *Going to* for plans.

e   Present simple to talk about timetables.

Focus
1   Complete the sentences using the correct form of the future of the verbs in brackets.

a   We ..*are going to visit*.. (visit) the science museum tomorrow. (intention)

b   I .... (go) to a football match tomorrow. (fixed plan)

c   School .... (start) at 8 a.m. next Monday. (timetable)

d   People .... (treat) by robots in the future. (passive)

e   People .... (not have) personal cars in the future. (prediction)

f   What kind of homes .... we .... (live) in 50 years from now? (prediction)

Practice

2 **Circle the best options to complete the comments.**

I think that more technology in the home **(will probably be)** / **probably will**[1] really useful for lots of people, but I worry that **it'll more difficult** / **it'll be more difficult**[2] for some older people to use. For example, my grandmother **won't be able to see** / **won't able to see**[3] some of the small controls on things. I hope tech designers **also will think** / **will also think**[4] about older people and people with disabilities.

Lots of things we do face-to-face now, like school and work meetings, **will be definitely done** / **will definitely be done**[5] online in the future. People **will routinely have** / **will have routinely**[6] appointments with specialist doctors in different cities and they **won't even have to** / **will even not have to**[7] leave home. However, we have to remember that lots of people in the world don't have reliable internet access and they **won't able to access** / **won't be able to access**[8] all those online services.

⦿ Get it right!

Remember that you always need a main verb after *will*, including *will be* + adjective.

Having less housework ***will be good*** *for busy parents.*

Adverbs usually come after *will* / *won't* and before other verbs.

A lot of routine jobs ***will probably be done*** *by machines.*

Challenge ⭐

3 **Complete the conversation using the verbs provided to express the future. Use *going to* for plans, *will* for predictions and present simple for timetabled events.**

A: What topic .... *are* .... you ... *going to choose* ...[1] (choose) for your technology report?

B: I ....[2] (do) research about homes in the future.

A: Really? What .... our homes ....[3] (be) like in the future?

B: I think they ....[4] (make) from organic material which absorbs heat for energy, so we ....[5] (not use) any gas or coal for heating.

A: That's interesting. I ....[6] (go) to a technology fair at the science museum on Saturday. Do you want to come?

B: What time .... it ....[7] (start)?

A: Doors ....[8] (open) at 9 a.m. Let's meet at ten to nine?

B: OK. See you there!

› 5.4 Have a story personalised!

1 Complete the conversation between two friends. What does Omar say to Victor?
For questions a–e, write the correct number 1–5.

Victor: I need to buy a present for my aunt's birthday. I don't know what to get.

Omar: a ....

Victor: She loves watching films.

Omar: b ....

Victor: No, that's too difficult. I don't know what she's seen.

Omar: c ....

Victor: That's not special enough, I want something more personal.

Omar: d ....

Victor: That's not a bad idea.

Omar: e ....

1 How about a poster of her favourite film?

2 What about a box set of her favourite films?

3 What sort of things does she like?

4 You could get her a gift token for streaming films online.

5 You could have it personalised online.

2 Complete the sentences using *too, too much* or *too many*.

a Alex spends ....*too much*....... time playing computer games.

b Neema bought some shoes, but they are .... small for her.

c Katrina wanted to go into the coffee shop, but there were .... people.

d Jason tried to solve the puzzle, but it was .... difficult for him.

e Yasmin wanted to go out with her friends, but she had .... homework.

> 5.5 Technology meets archaeology

1 **Label the photos with one word from each box.**

| Greek   Islamic   Ottoman   Roman |

| helmet   manuscript   statue   vase |

a

This civilisation originated in what is now known as Italy and spread to western Europe and northern Africa (1st century BCE to 5th century)

This is a ....

....

b

This civilisation originated in the eastern Mediterranean and spread to Central Asia (8th century BCE to 2nd century BCE)

This is a ....

....

c

This civilisation originated in the Anatolian Peninsula and spread to south-eastern Europe (14th century to early 20th century)

This is a ....

....

d

This civilisation originated in the Arabian Peninsula and spread to Central Asia (7th century CE to early 20th century)

This is a ....

....

Challenge

2 **Research one of the artefacts and answer these questions about it in your notebook.**

- What was it used for?

- What was it made from?

- What does it say about the skills of the people who created it?

⟩ 5.6 In ten years' time …

1　Read the opinions. Match the blog posts and the photos.

What will the world be like in ten years' time?

Hamid: I think that we won't be using gas and oil any more. We'll be using wind and solar energy. We won't be travelling in individual cars any more. We'll be travelling in multi-person self-driving electric vehicles. I don't think we'll be living in houses either. We'll be living in eco-pods that are energy-efficient and reduce our carbon footprint. …………

Gita: We won't be living in cities on land any more, because they'll be too crowded. In the future, we'll be living in underwater cities. We'll be growing food in underwater farms. We won't be eating fish or meat. We'll be eating seaweed and marine plants. We might go to the Earth's surface for holidays. …………

Anand: I think that robots will be doing most of our jobs. They'll be making our food and taking care of us in hospitals. We won't be travelling to school any more, because everyone will be studying at home! We'll still be using the internet to talk to each other, but instead of looking at a screen, we'll have holographic images, so it looks like you are really in the room with someone. …………

2　For each question, write the correct name.

Which of the writers …

a　talks about education? ……………

d　talks about transport? ……………

b　is worried about pollution? ……………

e　thinks that food will change? ……………

c　thinks communication will change?

……………

f　is worried about overpopulation?

……………

Challenge

3　Which of these writers do you agree with or disagree with? Choose two opinions and say why you agree or disagree. Write your answers in your notebook.

> # To have something done

Check!

1 Read the caption. Underline the past participle forms.

2 Complete the rules.

We can use .... ¹ + object + ... ²
participle to say that we asked someone to do
something for us.

In informal English, we can use *get* instead

of .... ³.

We can use a variety of tenses with this structure.

subject	*have* or *get*	object	past participle
She	*had / got*	*her hair*	*done.*

Here's a photo of my mother's sister on her wedding day. She had her hair and make-up done by a beautician. She had her hands decorated with henna. They had their portrait taken by a professional photographer. Don't they look lovely?

Focus

1 Complete the sentences using the correct tense of *have something done* and the words in brackets.

a You can *have your T-shirt personalised* . (T-shirt /personalise)

b My parents are looking for a builder. We need ....
(garden wall /repair)

c I am going to the photography studio tomorrow. I ....
(my photo /take)

d We didn't go to the supermarket last week. We ....
(our food /deliver)

e I dropped my phone and I .... (it /not repair) yet.

f My brother is at the dentist at the moment. He ....

(a tooth /extract)

Practice

2 Correct the mistakes. One sentence is correct.

a   I'm going to get ~~repaired my bike~~ *my bike repaired* at the bike shop.

b   We're having a new cooker installed tomorrow.

c   Jake had to having his coat dry-cleaned last week.

d   We're having a special cake to be made for my mum's birthday.

e   I hate going to the dentist so I didn't my teeth checked for a whole year.

Challenge

3 Complete the sentences or questions using *have something done* and words from the box. Use the correct tense.

a new suit / make	eyes / test	room / paint
it / repair	the sink / not replace	your hair / cut

a   **A:** I went to the optician's yesterday.

    B: Did you *have your eyes tested* ?

b   **A:** I had to clean out my room because the painters are coming tomorrow.

    B: Are you ....?

c   **A:** The screen on my phone is broken.

    B: I think you should ....

d   **A:** I'm at the hairdresser's right now.

    B: Are you ....?

e   **A:** Mark went to the tailor's last week.

    B: Did he ....?

f   **A:** The water pipe is leaking!

    B: Yes, I know. We ....
.... yet.

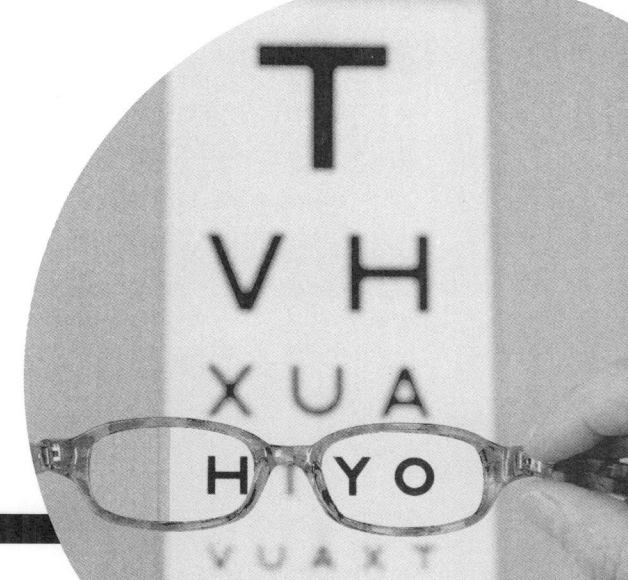

⟩ Future continuous

Use of English

Check!

1 Read the caption. Underline examples of the future continuous.

2 Choose the correct words.

We use the future continuous for events that will be *finished / in progress*[1] at a future time.

We form the future continuous by using will + *be* + the *present / past*[2] participle.

'We won't be living in houses and flats any more. We'll be living in small eco-pods that we can move around from place to place. No one will be driving cars on the road. Everyone will be using flying cars instead.'

Focus

1 Complete the sentences using the future continuous and information from the caption.

a We ....*will be living*.... (live) in eco-pods.

b Everyone .... (travel) in flying cars.

c We .... (not drive) in cars any more.

d People .... (not eat) meat in their diets any more.

e What kind of diet .... people .... (eat)?

f .... everyone .... (use) solar and wind-based energy?

Get it right!

Remember that we use other future forms for:

- states and situations that will exist at a future time

  Most car parks **will have** charging points for electric cars. ✓

  Most car parks **will be having** charging points for electric cars. ✗

- things that will be normal or done regularly at a future time.

  In 20 years' time, people **will only use** electric cars for long journeys. ✓

  In 20 years' time, people **will only be using** electric cars for long journeys. ✗

Practice

2 **Complete the texts using a future form of the verb in brackets.**

Cities of the future ....*will have*........ [1] (have) far more space for walking and cycling. Most children .... [2] (able to walk) to school safely, and commuters .... [3] (cycle) to work every day instead of driving. That means that the air .... [4] (be) much cleaner and we .... [5] (not breathe in) low-quality air any more.

As a result of rewilding, in ten years' time this whole area .... [6] (be) forest again. Instead of open farmland, trees .... [7] (grow) where we're standing now. Local people .... [8] (earn) money from eco-tourism rather than farming and, hopefully, those tourists .... [9] (have) the opportunity to see all the wildlife that .... [10] (live) in the forest.

Challenge

3 **What are your predictions for your future in ten years' time? Write questions using the future continuous. Then write your own answers to them in your notebook.**

a   where / live? *Where will we be living?*

b   what / study? ....

c   what job / do? ....

d   where / work? ....

e   travel by plane? ....

f   use / money? ....

› 5.7 Improve your writing

1 What is your opinion about online learning? Complete the sentence with a reason for your opinion.

Online learning is a good idea because ....

....

2 Match descriptions a–f to sentences 1–6.

a Introduce your report by saying how it is organised. [6]

b Give examples to illustrate your argument. [   ]

c Start with the positive aspects. [   ]

d Link your arguments by using connectives. [   ]

e Show that you have done some research. [   ]

f Predict future developments. [   ]

---

1 It is likely that online learning will be combined with classroom teaching.

2 Many students use self-learning study tools such as apps.

3 On the other hand, a disadvantage could be that students don't develop enough social skills.

4 Online learning is fun and interesting, and you learn to use different computer programs.

5 Recent studies have shown that online learning encourages students to be more independent.

6 ~~We have divided our report into three sections.~~

---

3 Read the beginning of the report. Then make notes in your notebook under each heading. Use your notes to write a report in your notebook.

Report on online learning

Introduction

We have divided our report into three sections. The first section describes different types of online learning. The second section explains some of the advantages and disadvantages. The third section makes some predictions about how online learning is likely to develop in the future.

1 Different types of online learning

2 Advantages and disadvantages of online learning

3 Future developments

› 5.8 Non-fiction

The Antikythera Mechanism

Around the 2nd century BCE, a ship on its way from Greece to Rome sank in the Adriatic near the island of Antikythera. Two thousand years later, the shipwreck was discovered by Greek sponge divers. They found a treasure trove of beautiful vases, pots, jewellery and statues. The strangest thing they found was a wooden box containing many bronze fragments of gears and dials that interconnected like the wheels of an old-fashioned mechanical clock.

Researchers used X-rays and 3D imaging methods to analyse the fragments. They concluded that the device in the box had been used as a kind of calendar to determine the positions of the sun and the moon. Some inscriptions showed that it had also been used to display the positions of the planets as they moved across the sky. When you set the main gear to a certain calendar date, you could find out where the planets would be in the sky on that date. It was an early form of mechanical computer.

For 2000 years, the device lay under the sea. The technology that created it was lost. It was not until the 16th century that technology again managed to attain the same level of precision.

1   Read the text. Using a dictionary to help you, find words in the passage to match these meanings.

    a   Small pieces ....

    b   Valuable objects ....

    c   Accuracy ....

    d   Circular disc ....

2   Answer these questions. Answer question b in your notebook.

    a   What makes the Antikythera mechanism so special?

        A   It shows an advanced level of engineering.

        B   It was lost for a long time underwater.

        C   It was difficult to understand how it worked.

    b   What does this discovery tell us about the people who made this object?

3   Imagine you saw this mechanism in a museum. In your notebook, write a diary entry about your impressions.

6 ▶ Rules and laws

> 6.1 School rules

1 Complete the questions in the speech bubbles with words from the box.

behaviour	break	detention	respect
stay behind	~~strict~~	trouble	warning

1 Do you have a lot of rules in your school? Is your school very ....*strict*..........?

2 I think our school has a lot of rules, but they're mainly good ones. You mustn't shout or run in the corridors, for example. I think that's to show .... for others.

3 Another rule is that if you're absent you're expected to bring a note from your parents, or you'll get into ....

4 We get plus points for good .... every week and it goes on our report. I think that's good, because it encourages us to behave well.

5 Yes, if you .... the rules you get minus points, or you have to .... after school.

6 The teachers are quite nice though. Before they give you a detention, they always give you a verbal ....

7 That's right! After three warnings, you get a ....!

2 **What is your opinion about rules in your school? Complete the sentences in your notebook with your own ideas.**

    a   I think school rules are important because …

    b   One important rule is …

    c   One rule I would change is …

Challenge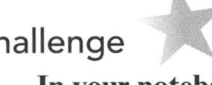

3 **In your notebook, make a list of three new rules for your school or class. Say how they will improve student behaviour.**

> 6.2 Family life

1 Read the article. Use words from the box to complete the gaps.

as (×2) be for in like of sure your to

Managing your time

In order to make the best use of your time, it's a good idea ....*to*........[1] review your **productivity** regularly. This means looking at all the activities you do during the day and making ....[2] that you are doing them as efficiently ....[3] possible.

Many large companies have a **system** for reviewing **employee** productivity, and company **executives** are usually trained to include this ....[4] their management practice. But this **process** can also ....[5] applied to studying, as well ....[6] everyday household tasks ....[7] cleaning and cooking.

An important first step is to **set** realistic **goals**. Make a list ....[8] tasks and decide which ones are most important. Make a schedule ....[9] when you can reasonably complete each goal. Breaking your **workload** down into small steps can reduce stress and give you added motivation as you complete each step.

Remember to plan for breaks as well! If you study for too long without a break, ...[10] concentration will reduce and your productivity will decrease!

2 Look at the words in bold in Exercise 1. Match them with the definitions.

a A series of steps. ...... *process* ....

b Amount of work. ....

c Does things quickly without wasting time. ....

d How much you achieve in a certain time period. ....

e Senior managers who make important decisions in a company. ....

f A set way of doing things. ....

g People who work for a company. ....

> 6.3 House rules

1 Read the blogs. Which rules are the same in your home?

Tell us about rules in your home. Do you have a lot of rules? Do you agree with them?

Leila The main rules in our home are about keeping our bedrooms tidy and making our beds. My brother and I take turns cleaning the bathroom and doing the vacuuming. Everyone wears slippers when they're in the house, so it's not that bad.

Nabil My dad's very strict about me getting all my homework done, so that's always first. I'm not allowed to watch TV or look at my phone until my homework is done. There isn't a complete ban on phones, but my dad gets annoyed if I look at it too often!

Danuta I always have to tell my parents where I'm going, who I'm with and what time I'll be home. Sometimes it's really awkward when my friends are staying out late, but I always have to be back before 9 p.m. If I want to go anywhere, I always have to make sure my parents are OK with it first.

2 For each question, write the correct name: Leila, Nabil, Danuta.
Which writer talks about the following?

a Rules for going out. ....*Danuta*........

b Household chores. ....

c Screen time. ....

d Not wearing shoes at home. ....

e Asking permission. ....

f Studying. ....

3 In your notebook, write answers to the questions in the blog title.

Study tip

When you look for the answers to questions, look for words in the text with a similar meaning. For example, making beds and cleaning are types of household chores. Find other words in the text that have a similar meaning to words in the questions.

⟩ Verbs in the passive followed by the infinitive

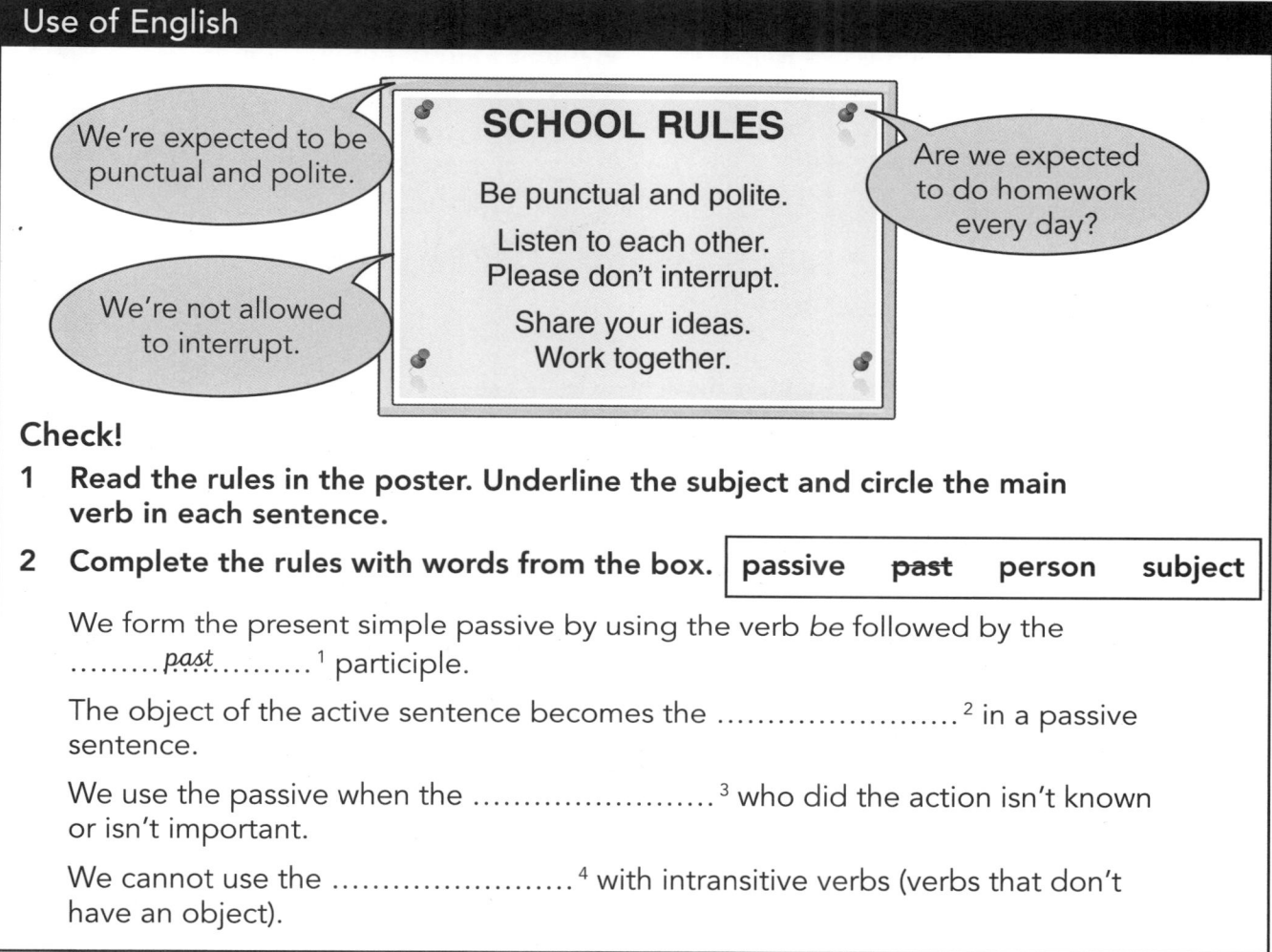

Check!

1   Read the rules in the poster. **Underline the subject** and **circle the main verb** in each sentence.

2   Complete the rules with words from the box. | passive   ~~past~~   person   subject |

We form the present simple passive by using the verb *be* followed by the ....*past*.........¹ participle.

The object of the active sentence becomes the ....² in a passive sentence.

We use the passive when the ....³ who did the action isn't known or isn't important.

We cannot use the ....⁴ with intransitive verbs (verbs that don't have an object).

Focus

1   **Complete these sentences using the present simple passive of the verbs in brackets.**

   a   You .*are encouraged to do*. (encourage, do) two hours of homework every day.

   b   They .... (expect, wear) a school uniform.

   c   We .... (ask, send) our homework by email.

   d   I .... (expect, read) four books every month.

   e   How teenagers spend their time .... (think, be) important for brain development.

   f   My brother .... (not allow) to use his mobile phone in class.

Practice

⊙ Get it right!

Remember that we use a passive followed by an infinitive in the expression *to be supposed to do*, to say that something is meant to happen, sometimes when the opposite is actually true.

*The lesson **is supposed to start** at 9.30, but we're always five minutes late.*

*We**'re not supposed to tell** anyone about it – it's a secret.*

We use the active form of the verb *I suppose* to mean *I think / guess*.

***I suppose** that's why she didn't come.*

2   Choose the correct option to complete the sentences.

a   We should go now – *I'm supposed to be* / *I suppose to be* home by six o'clock.

b   Be careful, *we don't suppose to use* / *we're not supposed to use* our phones in class.

c   Do you want to borrow my book? *I'm supposed so.* / *I suppose so.* But I need it back by Friday.

d   You know the trip on Monday – *do we suppose to take* / *are we supposed to take* our own lunch?

Challenge ⭐

3   Use the words to make questions. Then, in your notebook, answer the questions about your school.

a   What kind of clothes / you / expect / wear

What kind of clothes are you expected to wear?

b   students / ask / work in groups?

....

c   doing projects / think / be / a good way to learn?

....

d   you / expect / collaborate or compete?

....

e   What books / you / encourage / read?

....

f   How many hours / you / expect / study / every day?

....

› Reported questions and statements

Use of English

Salma: Where's Fatima? She said she'd be here at 4 p.m[1]. She asked me to wait for her at the school gate[2] and told me not to be late[3]!

Aisha: It's OK, Salma, calm down. Fatima told me that she had to stay late after class today[4]. She asked me if I was going to see you[5] and ...

Check!

1 **Read the conversation. Write the correct numbers.**

    a   Two reported statements. [*1*], [   ]

    b   Two reported questions. [   ], [   ]

    c   A reported command. [   ]

2 **Read the grammar explanation. Complete the chart.**

When we report a statement or a question, we change the tense and any necessary pronouns.

Remember to use a personal object pronoun after *tell*, but <u>not</u> after *say*. (*She told me that she was busy. She said ~~me~~ she was busy.*) It is also possible to use a pronoun after *ask*. *She asked (me) if I was busy.*

Tense changes in reported speech	
Present simple	1 *Past simple* ....
Present continuous	2 ....
Present perfect	3 ....
will	4 ....
can	5 ....

For reported questions, we use subject–verb order (not verb–subject order as in direct questions). *She asked if I was going to be late.* (NOT: ~~She asked if was I going to be late.~~)

For reported commands and requests, we use *tell / ask* + pronoun + infinitive.

Focus

1 **Write the original words that were spoken.**

   a She said she'd meet me at 4 p.m.

     'I *ll meet you* .... at 4 p.m.'

   b She asked me to wait for her at the school gate.

     'Please .... at the school gate.'

   c She told me not to be late.

     'Please .... late.'

   d She told me that she had to stay late after class today.

     'I .... stay late after class today.'

   e She asked me if I was going to see you.

     '.............................. to see Salma?'

> ### ⊙ Get it right!
>
> Remember that we often use *say* or *mention* to report something written. We use *it* as the subject of an active reporting verb to refer to the text, not the writer: *It* (= the article/advert) *said that …*
>
> *On the website, it mentioned that under 16s could get in for half price.*
>
> *In the article, it said that 59 per cent of the global population were active internet users.*
>
> *In her message, she said that she was running a bit late.*

Practice

2 **Choose the best reporting option to complete the sentences.**

   a The article *mentioned* / *wrote* that the family had followed a different schedule.

   b In his email, he *said* / *told* that he had already booked a place to stay.

   c In the directions, it *didn't say* / *wasn't said* where we could park.

   d I loved it, but my parents *said* / *told* that it was too expensive.

   e The advert *didn't mention* / *didn't tell* how much the tickets were.

   f Adam *asked* / *requested* me to help him get the food ready.

Challenge

3 **Rewrite the conversation in your notebook using reported speech.**

Jason:	Can I go over to my friend's house after school?
Jason's mother:	Who do you want to visit?
Jason:	I want to go over to Luke's. We're doing a school project together.
Jason's mother:	OK, that's fine, but please phone me when you get there.
Jason:	Thanks, Mum! How long can I stay?
Jason's mother:	Don't be any later than 7 p.m.

> 6.4 Doing the right thing

1 **Read the descriptions of the situations. For each one answer:**

Would you have done the same? ....

....

....

If not, what would you have done? ....

....

....

What wouldn't you have done? ....

....

....

Give reasons for your answers. ....

....

....

a Magda was walking home along her street when she saw a man trying to look through the window of a car. At first, she thought he was trying to see what the time was. After a couple of minutes, she saw him trying the door handle of the car. Magda realised the man was locked out of the car. She was late for her violin lesson and didn't stop to help because she didn't know what she could do. She walked home quickly and told her dad, who went out to help.

b Jamal was waiting at the bus stop on his way to school when he noticed a man going into the front garden of the house on the opposite side of the road. He didn't go to the front door, but he went round the side of the house and started climbing over the gate into the back garden. Just then, the bus arrived so Jamal didn't do anything and he got on the bus.

c Reza was in the school playground with his friends when he saw a group of three boys making fun of a younger boy. They'd taken his school bag and were throwing it to each other. The boy was clearly upset. Reza was worried about him and phoned the school office to tell them what was happening.

> 6.5 Rights and responsibilities

1 Complete the texts with words from the box.

a bank account	blood	do	full-time	give	home	joined
jury duty	learned	left	open	part-time	the army	to drive
to vote	was working	donate				

The first thing I did when I got my first job was to .... ¹. I was only 15 and I only had a .... ² job at the local newsagent on Saturdays, but I think it is important to keep track of your earnings, especially if you want to save up for something special.

I .... ³ when I was 17 because I wanted to learn a trade and couldn't afford to go to college or training school. It was tough but I .... ⁴ a lorry and got good training as a mechanic. I'd recommend it as a good way to get started in your career.

I was really happy when I was old enough .... ⁶ in the general election. It makes you feel like an important part of society.

I .... ⁵ when I was 18 and went off to university. To begin with, I really missed my family and was so homesick! But after the first term, I started to enjoy my independence. I think it's a big step to becoming an adult.

I was called up to .... ⁷ last year. I .... ⁸, so I had to get permission to take time off work. It was a case about someone who had collected money for a charity but didn't use the money as he had promised. I didn't really enjoy it, but I think it's an important service that every citizen should do if they can.

There are several reasons to .... ⁹. Firstly, you can help people who are sick or have been in an accident. Secondly, you can get a free medical check. Thirdly, it sets a good example to other people and encourages them to do the same. I think everyone should do this every year as soon as they are old enough.

2 Which of these opinions do you agree with? Choose two of these actions and explain why you will or won't do them in the future. Write in your notebook.

> 6.6 What happened?

1 **Look at the photo. Look carefully at each person and identify what they look like, what they are doing, what they are wearing.**

2 **Cover the photo with a sheet of paper. Read the witness account of the scene. Underline the ten mistakes and correct them.**

I was walking through the pedestrian zone. It was crowded and a lot of people were doing their shopping. It was raining. People were riding bikes on one side of the road. A woman with dark hair was riding her bike towards me. She was wearing a long scarf and a long coat. Behind her on the right was a man on a bike. He was wearing a helmet. Behind her on the left was a woman with short hair and glasses who was also riding a bike. A man and a teenager were standing on the left. The man was wearing a jacket and a hat and the teenager was wearing trousers and boots. They were eating a sandwich and some snacks.

3 **Uncover the photo. Check your corrections.**

> # Third conditional

> If only I hadn't played football with my friend this morning. If I hadn't played football, I would've been on time for lessons. And I wouldn't have got this detention!

Use of English

Check!

Complete the rules with words from the box.

imaginary	only	perfect	would

We use the third conditional to talk about ....¹ past situations.

In the *if* clause we use the past ....² form of the verb.

In the main clause we use ....³ + *have* + past participle.

The *if* clause can be first or second, without any change of meaning.

If I had got up earlier, I wouldn't have missed the bus.

I wouldn't have missed the bus if I had got up earlier.

We can use the *if* clause with *if* ....⁴ or *I wish* to express regret.

If only I had got up earlier. / I wish I had got up earlier.

Focus

1 **Read the rules. Answer the questions with yes or no.**

a Did the boy play football this morning? ....

b Was he on time for his lessons? ....

c Did he get a detention? ....

2 **Circle the correct words.**

a If I **had** / **would have** studied more, I **had** / **would have** passed the test.

b You **had** / **would have** won the match if you **had** / **would have** practised more.

c   They **wouldn't have / hadn't** called the doctor if they **hadn't / wouldn't have** been worried.

d   If Marie **had / would** listened more carefully, she **had / would have** chosen the right answer.

e   If we **hadn't / wouldn't** checked our email, we **hadn't / wouldn't** have known about the clothing sale.

f   If only I **had / hadn't forgot / forgotten** my house keys this morning!

g   I wish we **had / hadn't worn / wore** our warm coats. It's freezing in here.

Practice

3   Correct two mistakes in each sentence.

a   We wouldn't ^*have* gone to the station if we had know ^*n* about the rail strike.

b   If I hadn't in a hurry, I would had complained about the bill.

c   If Jake had left his bike outside, it wouldn't have damaged by the rain.

d   If we had saw the lost cat, we would have report it to the owners.

e   What you would have done if you had forgot your passport?

f   Would he have go to the dentist if he had break his tooth?

Challenge

4   Rewrite these sentences using the third conditional.

a   He didn't put money in the parking meter so he got a fine.

If he had .... *put money in the parking meter, he wouldn't have got a fine* ....

b   I had my phone with me, so I was able to call the emergency services.

If I hadn't ....

c   I didn't know you were in trouble, so I didn't help you.

If I had ....

d   He passed the test, so he got his driving licence.

If he hadn't ....

e   You looked out of the window and so you saw the birds escaping.

If you hadn't ....

> Past continuous

Use of English

Check!

Complete the rules a–c with words from the box.

background	intentions	interrupts
progress	same	scene

We were cycling along the main street. ☐
We were all wearing helmets. ☐ We weren't
going very fast. ☐ We were going to turn
right when suddenly a large lorry drove past
us into a side street on the right. ☐

a   We use the past continuous to describe
a .... ¹ or to give
.... ² information.

b   We often use the past continuous and
the past simple in the .... ³
sentence. We use the past continuous for an action in .... ⁴ and the past
simple for an action which .... ⁵ it.

c   We use the past continuous form of *be going to* for past .... ⁶.

Focus

1   Match the past continuous examples in the caption with the rules.
Write a, b or c in the boxes.

2   Choose the best verb form to complete the sentences.

    a   I *walked /* *was walking* to school when suddenly I *saw /* *was seeing* a rabbit.

    b   The cars *stopped / were stopping*, because some schoolchildren *crossed /*
were crossing the road.

    c   It was a beautiful day; the sun *shone / was shining* and the birds *sang /*
were singing.

    d   As soon as the school bell *rang / was ringing*, everyone *went / was going* to
the cafeteria.

    e   We *went / were going to go* to the park to play football, but it was too cold.

    f   They *didn't stand / weren't standing* at the bus stop, so the bus *drove / was*
driving past them.

Practice

3 Read the conversations. Underline any verbs that could be changed to use the past continuous. Write the correct form above the underlined verbs.

a **A:** Did you go anywhere last weekend?

   B: It rained so we played computer games at home.

b **A:** Why didn't you meet me after school yesterday? I waited for you.

   B: Sorry! I talked to the teacher about my project.

c **A:** I saw you on the bus yesterday. Where did you go?

   B: I went to visit my grandma, but she phoned to say she wasn't well, so I went shopping instead.

d **A:** I rode my bike yesterday when I ran into a tree.

   B: Oh no! What did you do?

Challenge

4 Write the verbs in the past continuous or the simple past.

a He .... (sit) under an apple tree when an apple
.... (fall) on his head.

b When she .... (arrive) at the cafe, she was
disappointed that her friends .... (not wait) for her.

c While they .... (play) football in the park, it
.... (start) to rain.

d My parents .... (live) in Japan when they
.... (meet).

e What .... (do) you .... (say)
when you .... (win) the prize?

f We .... (go) to buy you some flowers but we
.... (not have) time.

> 6.7 Improve your writing

1 Read the email. Match the questions with the topics.

> Asking questions   Break time
> Giving feedback   Group work
> ~~Technology~~

Dear Leila,

I'm writing to you because we're doing a project about classroom rules in schools around the world. I would be very grateful if you could tell me about your school by answering some or all of the following questions.

....*Technology*.... [1] Are you allowed to use phones or the internet in class? When are you allowed to use your phone? When can you use the internet?

.... [2] Are you allowed to stay in the classroom at break time or do you have to go outside?

.... [3] Are you encouraged to work in groups or individually? How much time do you spend working in groups? How much time is on your own?

.... [4] Do you have to be quiet during the lesson? What do you do if you don't understand something? Are you expected to ask another student?

.... [5] Are you expected to give presentations to the class? Do other students comment on your presentation? What kind of rules are there about that?

I look forward to hearing from you and I'd appreciate any information you can send me.

Best wishes,

Jackie

Send

2 Reply to the email in your notebook by answering the questions.

〉6.8 Non-fiction

1 Many works of fiction are based on true stories. Read the information about Robinson Crusoe and Alexander Selkirk. What are the similarities and differences between the two stories?

Robinson Crusoe is a novel about a young Englishman who was stranded on a desert island in the Pacific for 28 years. His ship was destroyed in a storm and all the other sailors were drowned. The novel was written by Daniel Defoe, a British novelist, and it was published in 1719. The book is written in the style of a diary. The hero gives an account of his many adventures and how he managed to survive before eventually being rescued by a passing ship. At first, the book was published with the name of Robinson Crusoe as the author, so people thought it was a true story.

Although *Robinson Crusoe* is a work of fiction, it may have been based on a true story. This was the real-life experience of a man named Alexander Selkirk, a Scottish pirate who was sailing along the coast of South America in 1704. He became concerned about the physical condition of the ship and refused to continue the journey. So the captain left him on a small island with a supply of food and water where he lived alone for four years before being rescued. He later learned that the ship had sunk and most of the crew had drowned. Those few men who survived were sent to a Peruvian prison, where they died.

a What is the same? ....

b What is different? ....

2 Answer the questions.

a What do you think it would be like to be alone on a desert island for four years? What would you like or dislike about it?

....

....

b What kind of rules would you have to make in order to (i) keep yourself fit and healthy, (ii) stay positive, (iii) send signals for help?

....

....

3 Imagine that you are Robinson Crusoe in your first week as a castaway. Write a diary entry in your notebook. Use your answers from Exercise 2.

7 ▶ Competition

> 7.1 Team sports or individual sports?

1 Match the phrases with the tips.

Sports psychology: Tips for success

a Be confident.

b Be patient.

c Build strong relationships.

d Improve your communication skills.

e Concentrate.

f Deal with stress.

g Don't forget to relax.

h Have self-esteem.

i Develop physical strength.

j Respect other people's opinions.

1 Get to know your teammates.

2 Stay positive and aim for success.

3 Train every day to improve your fitness.

4 Learn how to manage anxiety.

5 Believe in yourself.

6 Talk about your feelings and opinions.

7 Don't worry if you don't see results immediately.

8 Schedule time for breaks and get plenty of sleep.

9 Prepare yourself mentally and focus on your goals.

10 Listen to advice from people who know you.

2 Circle the best words to complete the text.

I joined the school hockey team this year and it's great! We **train** / **coach**[1] twice a week, so I've really improved my physical **strength** / **stress**[2]. I get **up** / **on**[3] really well with the other team members. They're very supportive, which has improved my **self-esteem** / **respect**[4] a lot. I'm more **strong** / **confident**[5] when talking to people because my **communication** / **mental**[6] skills have improved. I used to feel nervous and stressed at school, but sport has helped me to feel more **patient** / **relaxed**[7] and I'm able to **concentrate** / **improve**[8] better on my schoolwork.

Challenge

3 What is your opinion about doing sport? Do you like it or dislike it? Why? How can it help you? Write a paragraph in your notebook.

〉 7.2 Try this!

1 **Choose the correct words.**

a Judo is a *contact / non-contact* sport because players push each other with their arms and legs.

b Swimming is a *contact / non-contact* sport because participants don't touch each other.

c Jogging is a *competitive / non-competitive* sport because participants don't usually win or lose.

d Football is a *competitive / non-competitive* sport because each side wants to win.

2 **Complete the descriptions with words from the box and identify the sports.**

defends	goals	opposing	players	score	~~team~~	teams

a There are 15 players in a ....*team*........[1]. Two teams throw and kick an oval-shaped ball. The players try to win by running with the ball towards the other end of the pitch. The opposing team ....[2] their side and tries to stop them. Players ....[3] points by putting the ball on the ground on the other side of the line.

The sport is ....

b There are two ....[4] of nine players. Each team takes turns to hit the ball with a bat and run all the way around four bases of a diamond-shaped field. Players who get all the way round score a run. The ....[5] team tries to catch the ball after it has been hit and land it on a base before the player is able to reach it.

The sport is ....

c Each team has 11 ....[6]. Two teams kick the ball around the pitch. The players can't touch the ball with their hands. They kick the ball into the opposing team's net in order to score ....[7].

The sport is ....

Challenge

3 **What is your favourite sport? Why do you like it? Write a paragraph in your notebook.**

> 7.3 To compete or not to compete?

1 **Complete the conversation between two friends. What does Deniz say to Ahmet? For questions a–e, write the correct number 1–5.**

Ahmet: Are you in the school football team this year?

Deniz: a .....5......

Ahmet: How's it going?

Deniz: b ....

Ahmet: Oh, I think that would turn me off. I don't like too much pressure.

Deniz: c ....

Ahmet: That's all very well, but it's not for me. I prefer non-competitive sports like running or cycling.

Deniz: d ....

Ahmet: Yes, I know, but I just do them for fun and to stay fit. I don't try to be faster than anyone else.

Deniz: e ....

1 It's fun. I mean, it's hard work and there's a lot of pressure to score goals.

2 OK. Let's go running together this weekend!

3 Those sports can be very competitive too, you know!

4 Yes, I agree it puts some people off. But it's a fact of life and you have to get used to it.

5 Yes, I am. We train every Wednesday and Friday.

2 **Replace the words in bold with expressions from the conversation in Exercise 1.**

a They **discouraged me from** ......*put me off*...... trying out for the school swimming team.

b **Everyone knows** .... that there are winners and losers.

c Doing team practice every week **is fine** ...., but you have to make time for schoolwork as well.

d I am **not interested in** .... sports that don't have any sort of competition.

❯ Past perfect simple and past perfect continuous

Use of English

Tennis timeline

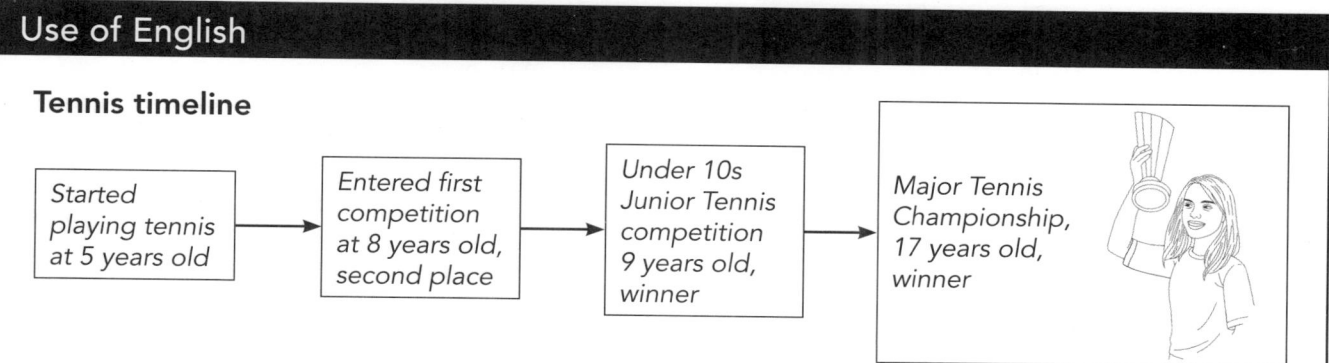

Underline the auxiliary verbs and circle the participles in the questions.

a How long <u>had</u> she <u>been</u> (playing) tennis before she won her first competition?

b How many competitions had she won before she won her first championship?

c Had she won any championships before winning a major championship?

d How long had she been playing before she won a major championship?

Check!

Underline the correct words in the rules.

We form the past perfect with had + **past** / **present**[1] participle.

We use the past perfect simple to describe a completed event or a period of time in the past that happened **before** / **after**[2] another event in the past.

We use the past perfect continuous to show that something was in **progress** / **completed**[3] before a time in the past.

Focus

1 Answer questions a–d in the Use of English box using the past perfect simple or continuous.

a ....

b ....

c ....

d ....

2 Choose the correct word to complete these sentences. Which ones are past perfect simple and which are past perfect continuous?

a I had been (climbing) / climbed for three hours before I reached the top of the mountain. *past perfect continuous*

b They weren't hungry because they had *eaten / eating* all the biscuits in the tin.

....

c Sula had been *thought / thinking* about taking up karate for quite a long time.

....

d We were late for the match, but luckily it hadn't *started / starting*.

....

e I couldn't go swimming because I hadn't *brought / bringing* my swimsuit.

....

Practice

3 **Correct the mistakes.**

        I'd
a ~~I've~~ trained for three years before attempting my first marathon last year.

b By the time she was 12, she had already been winning two gold medals.

c We hadn't never seen anyone who played football like him before.

d Had you had ever any doubts that you would win the race?

Challenge

4 **Complete the sentences and questions with the past perfect simple or continuous or the past simple.**

a We ......*were*...... tired because we ..*had been running*.. for two hours.

b They .... (not play) for long when our team .... (score) a goal.

c We .... (not go) the gym yesterday because we .... (forget) our trainers.

> Comparatives and superlatives

Use of English

	Jess	Zania	Lila
200 m sprint	35 seconds	39 seconds	33 seconds
Javelin throw	7 metres	9 metres	12 metres
High jump	2 metres	1.8 metres	1.9 metres

Jess runs faster than Zania, but is slower than Lila.
Zania is better than Jess at throwing but Lila throws the best.

Check!

1   Complete the sentences about Jess, Zania and Lila.

a   Jess isn't ......*as fast as*...... (fast) Lila in the 200 m sprint.

b   Lila is .... (fast) Zania.

c   Lila throws .... (far).

d   Jess can't throw the javelin .... (far) Zania.

e   Lila isn't .... (good) Jess at jumping.

f   Jess jumps .... (high).

g   Zania is .... (good) Jess at throwing.

2   Match the two parts of each rule for forming the comparative and the superlative.

a   For short adjectives,

b   For long adjectives,

c   To make negative comparisons,

d   To say things are equal or not equal,

e   To make comparative adverbs,

f   There are some irregular adjectives:

g   There are some irregular adverbs:

1   good – better – the best, bad – worse – the worst, far – further – the furthest

2   we add -er or -est to the adjective.

3   we use as … as or not as … as.

4   we use less in front of the adverb or adjective.

5   we use more and add -ly to the adjective.

6   we use more or the most.

7   well – better – best, badly – worse – the worst, far – further – the furthest.

Focus

1 Choose the correct words.

a Running a mountain marathon is *more / most* challenging than running a city marathon.

b Robin runs *faster / more faster* than the others.

c We were the most *successfully / successful* team of the season.

d Dania jumps *more highly / higher* than I can.

e Our teacher is less *strictly / strict* this year than last year.

f Your football team is playing *more badly / worse* than ours.

Practice

2 Complete the sentences using the pattern *as … as* with the adjective or adverb form of the word in brackets.

a Swimming can be just …*as energetic as*…. (energetic) running if you push yourself.

b We lost again, but we didn't play ……………………… (bad) last time.

c Momin can't run ……………………… (fast) Li, but he can keep going for longer.

d I love swimming in the pool, but it's

……………………… (fun) swimming in the sea.

Challenge

3 Write a second sentence that means the same as the first, using the word in brackets. Do you agree with these opinions?

a High jump is almost as difficult as long jump. (a bit)

Long jump is a bit more difficult than high jump.……

b Rugby and football are equally dangerous. (just)

……………………………………………………………………

c Runners are much stronger than cyclists. (not nearly)

……………………………………………………………………

d There is no sport that is more popular than football. (most)

……………………………………………………………………

> **⊙ Get it right!**
>
> Remember that we use the pattern **x is (not) as + adjective / adverb + as y** to say that:
>
> - x and y are roughly similar: *You can train outdoors **just as easily as** in the gym.* ✓
>   *You can train outdoors **as easy as** in the gym.* ✗
> - x is less good / boring, etc. than y: *Running in the countryside is **not as easy as** on a running machine.* ✓
>   *Running in the countryside is **not so easy as** like on a running machine.* ✗

＞ 7.4 Two competitions

1   Read the text. For each gap, circle the correct word from 1–8 below.

A National Spelling Bee

What are the .... ¹ difficult words to spell in English? Why do words like Wednesday and February sound so different from the .... ² they are spelled? If you sometimes misspell these words, you're not alone! But there are some teenagers who enjoy spelling difficult words. And many of them eagerly .... ³ part in a competition called a spelling bee.

Spelling bees are held in several countries around the world. The contest is usually for young people under the age of 16. To .... ⁴, contestants stand on a stage and are not allowed to consult books or the internet. The judge says a difficult word in English and the contestant is given two minutes to spell it.

The words get .... ⁵ and more difficult as the contestants progress from regional qualifying .... ⁶ through to the semi-final and final .... ⁷ of the contest.

The winner wins the title of Spelling Bee .... ⁸ and receives some money to be spent on their education.

1	much	*most*	many	more
2	way	how what	form	
3	put	have	take	give
4	contest	challenge	competition	compete
5	most	more	much	many
6	rounds	tests	questions	finals
7	stages	places	questions	judges
8	contestant	challenger	competitor	champion

Challenge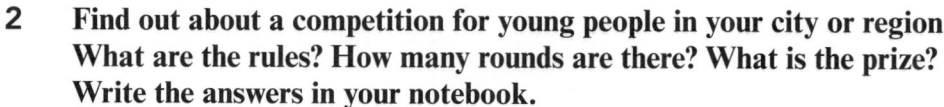

2   Find out about a competition for young people in your city or region. What are the rules? How many rounds are there? What is the prize? Write the answers in your notebook.

> 7.5 The art of photography

1   **Write the correct words next to each definition.**

background	flash	out of focus
silhouette	tripod	~~zoom lens~~

a   You can use this to take close-ups even if you're far away. .....*zoom lens*.....

b   It's behind the main focus of the photo. ....

c   You just see the outline of the subject. ....

d   The image isn't clear. It is a little unclear. ....

e   You stand your camera on this to hold it steady. ....

f   You use this to take a photo at night. ....

2   **Look at the photo. Choose the best words to complete the description. Write a caption.**

The photo was probably taken **with** / **without**¹ a zoom lens because it was taken from some distance away. The subject was moving rapidly so the photographer probably **used** / **didn't use**² a tripod. The snowboarder **is** / **isn't**³ shown as a silhouette. They are perfectly **in** / **out of**⁴ focus. There is a tree in the **background** / **foreground**⁵, to show how high up in the air the snowboarder is. The light is really bright, so the photographer probably **used** / **didn't use**⁶ a flash. A good caption for this photo would be ....

> 7.6 A towering achievement

1 Read about three sports in Brazil. Which one matches the photo? …………

A

Peteca is one of many traditional sports in Brazil. It was originally played by the indigenous people of Brazil centuries ago. Players have to hit a peteca, which consists of a piece of rubber with long feathers attached to it. The aim is to hit the peteca with your hand over a high net so that it lands in the opponent's court. The peteca can only be hit once on each side of the net. The sport can be played by two or four people.

B

It is said that the sport of **sandboard** was once enjoyed in Ancient Egypt, but it became popular among surfers in Brazil in the 1980s. When the waves weren't good enough for surfing, they decided to surf the sand. Nowadays, the boards – which look like snowboards – are specially designed to surf on sand. This is a fun activity for all ages anywhere there are sandy hills and dunes.

C

The sport of **capoeira** became popular in the early 20th century. It is a unique blend of martial arts, dance and acrobatics. Two opponents face each other within a circle of other players who accompany the fight with music and singing. The players use rocking dance-like movements to stay constantly on the move, thus avoiding attack. They also try to trick or mislead their opponent into leaving themselves open to attack.

2 For each question, write the correct letter A, B or C.

Which sport …

a is non-competitive? …………

b can be played by teams? …………

c is similar to a water sport? …………

d isn't played by two opponents? …………

e needs no special equipment? …………

f can be played only in certain locations? …………

g involves a large group of people? …………

h was invented less than 100 years ago? …………

Challenge

3 Which of these sports would you like to try?

> # Past perfect simple, active and passive

Use of English

After the race, he said that he had been encouraged by all the fans who had supported him for so long.

Check!

1   **Read the caption below the photo. Circle the verbs. Are they active or passive?**

2   **Complete the rules by circling the correct words.**

Active

subject	had	past participle of main verb
They	had	encouraged	him.

They   had   encouraged   him.

Passive

subject	had	past participle of be	past participle of main verb

He   had   been   encouraged   by his fans.

In ***an active / a passive***[1] sentence, the subject is the person or thing that does the action.

In ***an active / a passive***[2] sentence, the subject is the person or thing that receives the action. The person or thing that does the action is either unknown or obvious.

Remember that we ***can / cannot***[3] use the passive with intransitive verbs (verbs without objects).

Focus

1 **Choose the correct words.**

a We looked for our coach, but he had already *left* / *been left*.

b All our money had *spent* / *been spent* on tickets for the final.

c They hadn't *won* / *been won* a game for over a year.

d Everyone had *given* / *been given* a free ticket to see the game.

e He discovered that he had *awarded* / *been awarded* first prize.

f She said she hadn't *applied* / *been applied* to enter the competition.

Practice

2 **Complete the sentences with the past perfect active or passive of the verb in brackets.**

a Sami's uncle ....*had taught*.... (teach) him to play tennis.

b They .... (given) new trainers for the match.

c How many matches .... (lost) before Saturday's win?

d My friends .... (encourage) me to enter the competition.

e She .... (tell) she should do more practice if she wanted to win.

Challenge

3 **Rewrite the questions or sentences using the past perfect passive.**

a They had scored ten goals by the end of the match.

Ten goals had been scored by the end of the match.

b They hadn't expected him to win the race.

....

c How many contestants had they interviewed?

....

d Had they told the fans about the cancellation?

....

e By half-time, they had sent three players off the field.

....

› Connectives

> It's raining so we're going to stay in the gym today. You can play basketball here or you can practise gymnastics. As soon as the bell rings, line up by the door. We'll go back to our classroom after you have changed your clothes in the locker rooms.

We use connectives to join parts of a sentence. Connectives can be used as follows.

- To show additional ideas.

  *We watched the match **and** chatted with our friends.*

- To show alternative ideas.

  *We can have a break now **or** we can play another game.*

- To show contrasting ideas.

  *My sister loves football, **but** she doesn't like rugby.*

- To show cause or effect.

  *He won the match **because** he was faster than the other player.*

  *He hurt his knee **so** he couldn't play in the match.*

- To show purpose.

  *We got up early **so that** we wouldn't miss the bus.*

- To show sequence of time.

  *They practised for 20 minutes **before** the game started.*

Check!

1   **Look at the picture and read what the PE teacher says. Underline the connectives. What type of connective is each one?** ....

2   **Underline the connectives in these sentences. What type are they?**

    a   He didn't win the race although he had been training for several weeks.

    b   She is not only good at skateboarding, she is also an excellent skier.

    c   I didn't start riding a bike until I was eight years old.

    d   We turned on the TV in order to watch the championship final.

Focus

1 **Choose the correct word. Tick (✓) the sentences that can reverse the order of their clauses.**

 a They stopped the match *before /* (*because*) two players were injured. ☐

 b The spectators cheered *when / although* their team scored a goal. ☐

 c We wanted to buy tickets *but / and* they had already sold out. ☐

 d I didn't learn to ride a bike *until / as soon as* I was ten years old. ☐

Practice

2 **Join these sentences using connectives from the box.**

although	~~because~~	or	so

 a They couldn't play football. It was raining.

 They couldn't play football because it was raining.

 b We didn't have a snowboard. My dad made one out of a piece of plastic.

 ....

 c We didn't have a front row seat. We could see the players very well.

 ....

 d You can play basketball in the gym. You can play football outside.

 ....

> ### Get it right!
>
> Remember that:
>
> - We use **and** to connect ideas within a sentence. When there are three or more items or ideas, *and* usually comes before the last one.
>
>   *He mostly photographs* <u>animals</u>, <u>birds</u> **and** <u>landscapes</u>.
>
> - We use **because** to connect cause and effect ideas *within* a sentence.
>
>   *The judges awarded her first prize* **because** *her entry was so creative.*

Challenge ⭐

3 **Use the notes to write sentences in your notebook about these activities. Use connectives to join the ideas together.**

 a Running: good for fitness – no special equipment – can do any time.

 *Running is good for fitness, requires no special equipment **and** you can do it any time.*

 b Football: fun – good way to keep fit – need at least ten people to play.

 c Yoga: good for older people / people with injuries – gentle / go at own pace.

 d Snowboarding: fun / exciting – expensive equipment – need snow!

› 7.7 Improve your writing

1 **Read the question. Write your opinion.**

Are footballers paid too much?

....

2 **Complete the sentences with connectives from the box.**

~~Although~~	because	First	however	In addition
In conclusion	On the other hand	Second	such as	

a ....*Although*........top footballers are paid a lot, their careers are usually quite short. They don't earn high salaries for long. .....*A*......

b They deserve to be paid a high salary .... they train a lot and it takes many years for them to reach such a high level in their sport. ....

c Footballers shouldn't be paid more than essential key workers .... doctors and surgeons. They are only playing a game, not saving lives. ....

d They deserve high salaries, for two reasons. ...., they provide entertainment for millions of people. ...., they are role models for young people. ....

e Footballers who get high salaries don't always use their money wisely.

........................, they sometimes spend money on silly things. ....

f Some people think that more money should be given to help young people in the sport. ...., the money is paid by team owners and clubs and it's up to them how they spend it. ....

g Football is one of the most popular sports in the world. ...., some people disagree with the fact that top footballers are paid extremely high salaries and earn millions in transfer fees. ....

h ...., I think that there are more arguments against paying such high salaries to footballers. In my opinion, they should donate some of their money to help young people in the sport. ....

3 **Read the sentences again. Identify arguments for (F), arguments against (A), one sentence from the introduction (I) and one sentence from the conclusion (C).**

4 **Use the sentences in Exercise 2 to write your own essay answering the question in Exercise 1 in your notebook. Add your own ideas and opinions.**

> 7.8 Non-fiction

Junko Tabei Masters the Mountains

The first female climber to reach the top of Mount Everest and the first woman to climb the Seven Summits (the tallest mountain on each of the seven continents), Junko Tabei overcame her fear and faced many challenges to become a world-famous mountaineer and an influential voice in the environmental movement.

This historical fiction story imagines Junko's experience as a child and how it inspired her later achievements.

"Who wants to go on a field trip to the mountains?" Mr. Watanabe asked his fourth-grade class.

Junko's hand shot up in the air. She wasn't sure why, since going to the mountains probably meant lots of hiking and climbing, and she was bad at sports. *Really* bad. PE was her least favourite subject at school. She couldn't do the gymnastics other kids could do, and she much preferred reading to running.

This is not a good idea, she thought. She lowered her hand and pretended to sweep her bangs out of her eyes. But she really did want to try. It sounded like fun. She raised her hand again and made herself keep it there. Her heart thumped wildly in her chest.

The teacher nodded and smiled at her. "Ms. Ishibashi. Excellent. Anyone else?"

Other students raised their hands, too. Two boys sitting in front of Junko smirked and whispered to each other. She could guess what they were saying: *There's no way Junko can climb a mountain. She's tiny and weak. Plus, she's a girl.*

Junko Tabei Masters the Mountains
by Rebel Girls

1   **This is the first part of the story about Junko Tabei. Read it and answer the questions in your notebook.**

   a   What facts do you learn about Junko in this part of the story?

   b   What can you infer about Junko's character?

   c   What kind of bias do her classmates have about girls?

   d   What do you think will happen to Junko on this trip?

2   **Think about these questions. Then write your responses in your notebook.**

   a   How would you feel in Junko's situation? Would you go on the field trip or not?

   b   Have you ever had any experience of being discouraged from trying something difficult? How did it make you feel?

8 ▶ The environment

> 8.1 Let's talk about the weather

1 **Choose the best words to complete the posts.**

⬤ It's cloudy here at the moment but there will be **sunny / short**[1] intervals later in the day. Temperatures will rise gradually and tomorrow afternoon will be warm and sunny with **light / clear**[2] skies throughout the day.  •••

⬤ Coastal **parts / areas**[3] may see considerable fog and mist in the morning, which will clear up by midday. There's a chance of some light snow on high **places / ground**[4]. Winds will increase in strength, and there is a danger of **strong / big**[5] winds in the afternoon.  •••

⬤ After the recent dry spell, we'll be getting some **heavy / strong**[6] rain tomorrow afternoon. **Good / Hot**[7] news for gardeners! The rain will gradually decrease to just a few **small / light**[8] showers by the evening.  •••

⬤ Temperatures will be below freezing overnight, so there's a **good / large**[9] chance of some heavy frost in the morning. Watch out for icy **places / conditions**[10] on the roads.  •••

2 **Complete the sentences with phrases from Exercise 1.**

a Take an umbrella and raincoat. The forecast says <u>heavy rain</u> .

b Be careful riding your bike! There may be i…………… c…………… on the roads.

c G…………… n…………… for surfers! There will be lots of big waves tomorrow.

d Flood warning. There will be severe flooding in c…………… a…………… .

e There will be c…………… s…………… all day – enjoy!

f There's a g…………… c…………… of a thunderstorm, so stay indoors.

Challenge

3 **Describe the weather where you are today. Write a blog post in your notebook.**

› 8.2 Global warming and climate change

1 Complete the text with words from the box.

| droughts | evaporates | floods | ~~atmosphere~~ | heatwaves |
| hurricanes | moisture | rays | reflected | temperatures |

What is the difference between **global warming** and **climate change**?

Global warming describes the changes that are taking place in the Earth's ....*atmosphere*.......[1] and in average surface temperatures of the Earth. Carbon dioxide and other gases, mainly produced by burning fossil fuels, prevent heat from the Sun's ....[2] from escaping. Instead of being ....[3] back into space, they increase the temperature of the Earth.

Climate change describes the effects of global warming on our planet and on weather conditions. Warmer oceans mean that water ....[4] more easily, contributing more ....[5] to the air. This causes more frequent and more extreme ....[6] and tornadoes. Heavy rain leads to the flooding of rivers.

Melting glaciers contribute to rising ocean levels, which cause ....[7] in coastal areas. Many island nations and coastal communities are disappearing under water.

Increased ....[8] affect the Earth in other ways. All around the world, extremely hot days are being recorded and ....[9] are not only more frequent, they also cover larger areas of both land and ocean. The lack of rain causes ....[10], which means that people cannot grow enough food and there are more famines. In other countries, warm, dry conditions and strong winds cause massive forest fires that spread very quickly. The fires destroy trees, farms, houses and animal habitats.

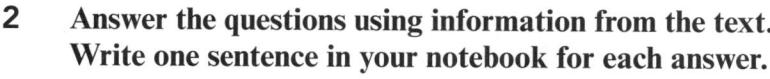

2 Answer the questions using information from the text. Write one sentence in your notebook for each answer.

a Why is climate change happening?

b How is climate change affecting the weather?

c How are these changes affecting people?

Challenge

3 What are some extreme weather events in your country? What are the causes and the effects? Write a paragraph in your notebook.

> 8.3 I'm very concerned about . . .

1 Read the blog posts. Tick (✓) the opinions that you agree with.

☐ **1** We throw away too much plastic. It **contaminates** the land and the water supply, and it harms birds and animals too. We should think of ways to avoid plastic packaging.

☐ **2** We should try to travel less by car, bus or plane and reduce our consumption of **fossil fuels**. We need to develop more alternative types of **renewable energy** instead and use environmentally friendly forms of transport.

☐ **3** I read that barely 10 per cent of **electronic devices** get recycled. We should find a way to recycle them safely and reuse the precious metals they contain.

☐ **4** I'm worried about global warming and the effects of climate change. Lots of animal species, such as polar bears and tigers, are losing their habitats and will disappear forever.

☐ **5** Extreme weather is getting more common everywhere in the world. Disasters caused by storms, floods and fires affect thousands of people and we should all try to do something to stop them from happening.

☐ **6** I think people **consume** too many things without asking whether they are ethically produced. I think we need to look for things that are grown or produced in a **sustainable** way.

2 Match the words in bold in the blog posts with the definitions a–f.

a Wind, solar or hydropower. ...*renewable energy*..

b Buy or eat. ....

c Petrol, gas and oil. ....

d Phones, laptops and computers. ....

e Poison or cause harm. ....

f Doesn't damage the environment. ....

3 Read the blog posts again. Which post is by someone who:

a is worried about pollution? ....

b thinks we should buy less? ....

c is concerned about species extinction? ....

d thinks we should stop buying single-use containers? ....

e wants more cooperation between people? ....

f wants to reduce consumption? ....

> Adverbs of frequency

Use of English

Sonia: Does it usually rain a lot in the winter?

Maleka: It hardly ever rains in the winter. It normally rains a lot in June and July.

Sonia: Are temperatures sometimes high in May?

Maleka: Yes! This year it has often been over 25 degrees. Sometimes it even reaches 35 degrees.

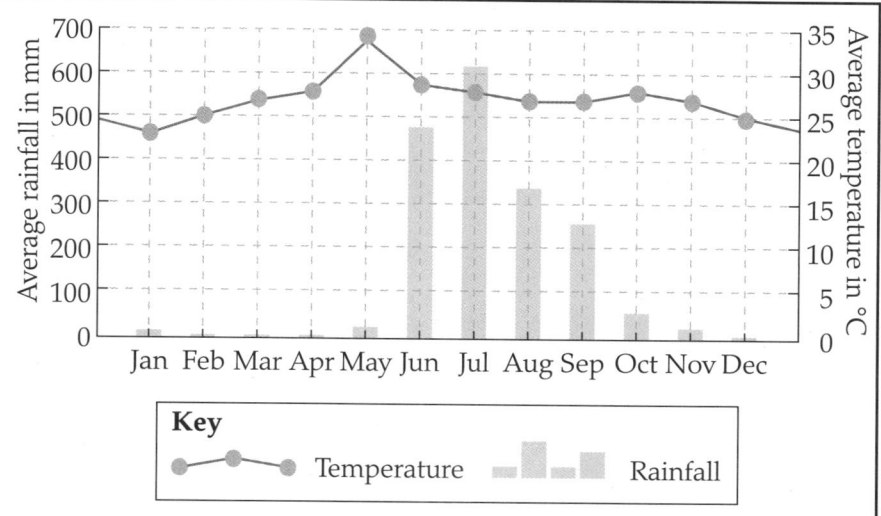

Key

●——●——● Temperature   ▮ ▮ ▮ Rainfall

Check!

1 **Read the conversation above. Circle the adverbs of frequency.**

2 **Complete the rules by circling the correct word.**

   a Adverbs of frequency tell us how **often / long** something happens.

   b The adverb goes **before / after** a main verb and **before / after** the verb *be*.

   c If there is an auxiliary, the adverb goes **after / before** the auxiliary and **before / after** the main verb.

   d *Occasionally* and *sometimes* can **also / never** be used at the beginning or at the end of a sentence.

3 **Add these words to the table. Some words have similar meanings.**

almost never   normally   hardly ever   occasionally   often   frequently   usually

0%	5–10%	10–30%	50%	60–70%	70–80%	100%
never	....	....	sometimes	....	....	always
	....			....	....	

Focus

1 **Choose the correct option.**

   a It *snows usually /* (*usually snows*) in the winter.

   b There *is often / often is* a lot of rain in the spring.

   c Floods *have frequently / frequently have* affected the coastal regions.

   d We *don't have usually / don't usually have* a lot of sunshine in the winter.

   e Our crops *are sometimes / sometime are* damaged by heavy frost in the spring.

   f Hurricanes *have almost never / almost have never* been seen in this region.

Practice

2 **Circle A, B or C to say where the adverb in brackets should go in each sentence. More than one answer may be possible.**

   a (more often) I think [A] we get [B] heavy snowfalls ([C]) than we did when I was little.

   b (occasionally) We have some pretty bad storms and [A] the power goes [B] off [C].

   c (sometimes) [A] When the monsoon rain is really heavy, the river [B] floods [C] the railway line.

   d (rarely) We have a tropical climate, so [A] the temperature [B] drops [C] below about 20 °C.

   e (more frequently) In recent years, the island [A] has [B] experienced [C] severe hurricanes [D].

> **⊙ Get it right!**
>
> Remember that some adverbs of frequency can go at the start of a sentence, such as *sometimes, occasionally.*
>
> **Sometimes**, *in winter, the lake freezes.*
>
> Adverbs of frequency can go at the end of a sentence, after the main verb and also after an object of the verb.
>
> *I think I <u>carry an umbrella</u>* **more often** *than I used to.*

Challenge

3 **In your notebook, answer the questions using the words provided. Then change the adverbs so that they are true for you.**

   a Do you ever go snowboarding? (hardly ever)
      I hardly ever go snowboarding in the mountains.

   b How often do you walk to school in the rain? (not often)

   c Have you ever been caught in a thunderstorm? (never)

   d What do you do at the weekend if it's sunny? (always)

   e What do you do at the weekend if it's raining? (usually)

   f Does the weather often affect your mood? How? (sometimes)

〉 Multi-word verbs

Cut down on plastic waste!

Don't throw away your plastic bags!

We're calling for all supermarkets to ban single-use plastic bags!

Check!

1   Circle the multi-word verbs in the magazine headline.

2   Read the rules. Answer the questions.

Multi-word verbs are verbs with two or three parts.

Sometimes the different parts of the verb can tell you the meaning. For example, *stand up, sit down, run away.*

Sometimes you can't guess the meaning from its parts and need to work out the meaning from context. For example, I'm **looking up** *a word* (which means *I'm looking for its meaning in a dictionary*).

Sometimes the particle adds emphasis or completeness to the verb. For example, *they* **used up** *all the paper* (**up** emphasises that the paper was completely used and none was left.)

   a   All multi-word verbs have two parts. ***True / False***

   b   Sometimes you need to work out the meaning from context. ***True / False***

   c   Sometimes the verb has a particular meaning that is different from its parts. ***True / False***

   d   Some verbs use *up* or *out* to make the verb stronger. ***True / False***

Focus

1   **Choose the correct words.**

   a   They are *cutting down* / *cutting down on* too many forests.

   b   We are ***running out of*** / ***running away from*** fossil fuels.

   c   Many marine animals will be ***wiped down*** / ***wiped out***.

   d   Oceans are ***warming up*** / ***warming down***.

   e   We need to ***look up*** / ***look after*** the natural resources of our planet.

Practice

> ### ⦿ Get it right!
>
> Remember how to use these single- and multi-word verbs correctly.
>
> - *Can you **cut** another slice of bread?*
> - *They **cut down** dozens of trees to build the new stadium.*
> - *We've **cut down on** the amount of meat we eat.*
> - *We **grow** a lot of vegetables in the garden.*
>
> - *George **grew up** in the countryside.*
> - *We need to find more creative ways to **save** energy.*
> - *She's **saving up** to buy a new bike.*
> - *Lots of people **use** their cars for short journeys.*
> - *It's a great recipe for **using up** leftover bread.*

2 Complete the text with a particle (*up, down, on,* etc.) in each gap. If no word is needed, put a dash (–).

> As a community, we've been trying to cut ...*down*... ¹ ....² waste and generally live more sustainably. A few of us have been walking to school instead of getting the bus. We saved ....³ the money we didn't spend on bus fares to buy a compost bin for our neighbourhood. We've also started growing ....⁴ our own vegetables. We're using recycled containers. So, for example, when someone uses ....⁵ a big tin of cooking oil, instead of throwing it ....⁶, we cut ....⁷ some holes in the bottom and use it to grow something in.

Challenge

3 Underline the multi-word verbs and replace them with a verb from the box that has the same meaning.

> | become extinct | destroy | get warmer | increase | ~~reduce~~ | support |

a   We want to <u>cut down</u> on our consumption of electricity. ....*reduce*........

b   Many species will die out unless we protect them. ....

c   The village was wiped out by the hurricane. ....

d   We need to scale up the use of renewable energy. ....

e   The Earth's atmosphere is heating up. ....

f   We must stand up for environmental issues. ....

4 Write three sentences in your notebook about what you can do for the environment. Use multi-word verbs from this lesson.

> ## 8.4 Zero waste

1 **Look at the title of the article. What kind of advice do you think it will give?**

a How to save money when shopping.

c How to have a healthier lifestyle.

b How to stop throwing plastic away.

d How to stop buying too much.

TIPS FOR
ZERØ WASTE SHOPPING

Have you ever gone into a supermarket and just looked at all the packaging? How many products aren't in plastic? Not .... [1]! Plastic keeps our food fresh and clean, but it's only used once and then it's thrown .... [2], and plastic takes hundreds of years to break down.

So here are some tips for zero waste shopping. First – and most important – bring your own .... [3] shopping bags. Some people use long-life plastic bags, but I prefer cotton .... [4] that are easy to wash and last forever. Try to .... [5] food that is wrapped in plastic. Bring your own bags for fruit and vegetables.

Second, always look carefully at the packaging and find out what it is made from. Choose products that are in a cardboard .... [6] or in a paper bag, like shampoo .... [7] and some kinds of deodorant. Choose products that are made from .... [8] materials, such as bamboo toothbrushes.

Finally, think carefully about what you buy. .... [9] buying water in plastic bottles, bring a water bottle from home. Use a glass or metal lunch box to bring food to school. Ask .... [10] if you really need to buy it or is it something you can make at home from simple ingredients? Now you're really on the path to zero waste!

2 **Read the article. For each gap, circle the correct word from 1–10 below.**

1 most more much (many)

2 off away up over

3 reusable accessible affordable usable

4 which ones types packages

5 avoid admit allow deny

6 box tin bottle tube

7 bottles tubes boxes bars

8 important natural cheap perfect

9 as well as despite instead of because of

10 someone every yourself one

3 **Copy the table into your notebook. Find words for containers and for materials in the article. Then add two more words to each category.**

Containers	Materials

> 8.5 Living and growing

1   Complete the sentences with words from the box.

consumer	food production	hydroponics	nitrogen
nutrients	pesticides	supply chain	vertical farming

a   A .... is a person who buys food from a shop and eats it.

b   The .... is the process by which food from a farm reaches consumers.

c   .... is the method of growing plants in water instead of in soil.

d   Plants take .... from the soil in order to grow.

e   .... is one of the essential nutrients that plants need to grow.

f   .... is the process of growing plants and raising animals for food.

g   .... is the method of growing plants for food in controlled conditions inside tall buildings.

h   .... are chemicals used to kill insects or weeds in order to improve production.

2   Match the two parts of each sentence. Which are advantages (A) and which are disadvantages (D) of urban farming?

a   People in cities

b   The food is fresher

c   Air in cities can

d   Urban farms are a wonderful way

e   Land may need to be

1   because it isn't transported over long distances. ....

2   can have access to healthier food. ......A.....

3   sometimes be polluted. ....

4   cleared of dangerous chemicals. ....

5   to bring communities together. ....

Challenge

3   Think of one more advantage and one more disadvantage of urban farming. Write your ideas in your notebook.

> 8.6 The air we breathe

1   Complete the posts with words from the box.

> cycle routes ~~low-emission zones~~ pedestrianised zone
> public transport system   urban forests

**What are some of the problems facing your town or city?
How could they be improved? Tell us your opinions.**

a   They should allow just electric cars in the city centre. They should create
....*low-emission zones*.... [   ]

b   I ride my bike to work every day, but cars just don't leave enough space for us on the roads. I'd like to see more
.... [   ]

c   I always have to wait ages for the bus. They're never on time and it makes

me late for school. We need a better
.... [   ]

d   We need more parks and trees everywhere in the city. It would help with carbon emissions too. We need more .... [   ]

e   I think that the centre of town should be closed to all vehicles. We need to have a
.... [   ]

2   Read the posts and answer the questions.

a   I love running, but the pollution is so bad, I always end up coughing.

b   It uses a lot of energy to heat and cool these offices. We need to do it without contributing to carbon emissions.

c   They should use solar and wind power to produce electricity.

d   Carbon emissions from cars are too high. Drivers should have to use alternative fuel.

e   Whatever the changes, they should be ones that will improve people's quality of life and health.

Who is concerned about the following?

1   using renewable energy ..*c*...

2   being carbon neutral ......

3   air quality ......

4   economic and social sustainability ......

5   electric vehicles ......

3   Number the ideas in Exercise 1 according to how effective you think they are for improving life in a city.

Challenge

4   Think of three ways to improve cities. Write your ideas in your notebook.

› Verbs followed by *-ing*

Use of English

This year we're planning to grow tomatoes, peas and green beans. We try to avoid using pesticides. We want to involve everyone from the local community, so don't forget to put your name on the list.

Check!

1 **Read the caption. Underline the *-ing* forms and the infinitives that follow a verb.**

2 **Complete the rules with words from the box.**

> the *-ing* form   *to* + infinitive   *to*

Some verbs are followed by .... [1].
For example: *avoid, consider, give up, suggest* and *imagine.*

Some verbs are followed by .... [2].
For example: *agree, decide, expect, hope, manage, plan, promise, want.*

Some verbs can be followed by either *-ing* or .... [3] and there is no difference in meaning. For example: *begin, continue, start, like, love, prefer.*

Focus

1 **Choose the correct words. If both are possible, circle both.**

a Our teacher suggested *bringing* / *to bring* our own water bottles to school.

b I'm going to start *growing* / *to grow* my own vegetables.

c Have you considered *to give* / *giving* up meat?

d They managed *to start* / *starting* an urban farm.

e I can't imagine *living* / *to live* without a phone.

f I've agreed *to help* / *helping* our neighbour with her garden.

Practice

2 Complete the sentences using the correct form of a verb from the box.

ask check find give give up
grow install produce reuse walk

a It's hard to imagine everyone .... *giving up* .... their cars and .... everywhere.

b It's worth .... the list of ingredients on the product or .... an assistant whether it contains added sugar.

c We had difficulty .... a suitable alternative to plastic packaging and then .... it at a reasonable cost.

d Have you considered .... students refillable water bottles and .... water fountains around the school?

e The article suggests .... your own herbs in plastic yogurt pots or .... old food tins.

Challenge ⭐

3 Complete the questions using the *-ing* or infinitive form of a verb from the box. Then answer the questions.

do drive learn make throw use

a Have you given up .... *using* .... plastic bottles yet? ....

b How can you avoid .... away plastic? ....

c Do you expect .... an electric car one day? ....

d Have you considered .... your own shopping bag? ....

e Have you decided .... more about global warming? ....

f What do you plan .... today to help the environment? ....

> Complex noun phrases

Use of English

Green Town Council

We're improving our city!

1 *We'll plant trees that will improve air quality.*
2 *We'll construct buildings made from recycled materials.*
3 *We'll have cars and buses that use solar energy.*
4 *We'll have many more outdoor public spaces.*
5 *We'll have streets with safe cycle routes.*
6 *Let's build a sustainable, energy-efficient city together!*

Check!

1 **Read the sentences in the information about a city. Underline the noun phrases. Circle the head nouns.**

2 **Read the explanations and examples below. Find an example of each type of noun phrase in the information about Green Town.**

A complex noun phrase consists of a head noun and other words to describe the noun. The head words are circled. The words describing it are underlined.

The words can go *before* the head noun.

Adjectives: We are developing <u>alternative renewable</u> (energy sources).

Determiners or quantifiers: <u>Many of these</u> (homes) use solar energy.

The words can go *after* the head noun.

A relative clause: We need to design (packaging) <u>that doesn't use plastic</u>.

A present participle clause: (People) <u>working on our farm</u> come from the local community.

A past participle clause: We prefer to use (shopping bags) <u>made from cotton or cloth</u>.

A phrase using a preposition: (Buildings) <u>with large windows</u> tend to waste energy.

Focus

1 **Write one word in each gap.**

a Recent advances ......*in*..... technology will reduce our energy consumption.

b Air pollution was caused by a large number .... factories in the region.

c People .... in this community decided to create a rooftop vegetable garden.

d We only buy products .... from recyclable materials.

e There are pedestrianised areas .... cars are not allowed to enter.

f Cities .... parks and trees tend to have better air quality.

Practice

2 **Choose the correct word to complete these noun phrases.**

a She'd read a lot and had a really detailed knowledge *about / of / on* the subject.

b Most students gave lack of time as their main reason *for / of / why* not walking to school.

c Nowadays, we tend to go online to find the answer *for / of / to* most questions we have.

d People are finding clever solutions *for / of / to* the situation.

Get it right!

Remember that we use specific / particular prepositions after some nouns when they are part of a noun phrase.

- *There isn't a simple **solution to** traffic congestion.*

- *We have to understand people's **reasons for** driving.*

- *She has an amazing **knowledge of** local plants and animals.*

Challenge

3 **Complete the second sentence so that it means the same as the first. Use the fewest words possible and avoid using relative clauses.**

a A lot of plastic goes into the ocean. It is harmful to marine life.

A lot of plastic ....*going into the ocean*........ is harmful to marine life.

b A number of factories are reducing carbon emissions. The number increased last year.

The number of factories .... increased last year.

c Our food is grown locally. It is fresher than food from the supermarket.

Food .... is fresher than food from the supermarket.

d Coal-fired electricity plants create a lot of greenhouse gases. They produce energy for our homes.

Coal-fired electricity plants .... create a lot of greenhouse gases.

e The solar panels generate all our electricity. They are on our roof.

The solar panels .... generate all our electricity.

f There was a beautiful park. It had lots of space for children to play.

There was a beautiful park .... for children to play.

> 8.7 Improve your writing

1 **Read the report. Match the paragraphs and these subheadings.**

1 A deadly hurricane .... **3** How hurricanes are formed ....

2 Future trends .... **4** Hurricane season ....

Deadly hurricane sweeps through the Bahamas

A	For residents of the Caribbean islands, the months from June to October are the most dangerous of the year. They call it hurricane season because every year an average of 15 tropical storms sweep through the region.
B	In recent years, the hurricane season has been starting as early as May. The hurricanes start as rotating areas of low pressure that increase in intensity as they move over warm water. These storms turn into hurricanes when they reach wind speeds of over 120 kph.
C	When Hurricane Dorian hit the Abacos Islands (just north of the Bahamas) in September 2019, its wind speed reached 298 kph. This Category 5 storm hovered over the Bahamas for three days, causing massive destruction. Wind, heavy rain and storm surges flooded towns and tore down houses and vegetation.
D	Meteorologists expect that hurricanes will get worse. As a result, it is thought that hurricanes of greater intensity and increased destruction are likely to become more common.

2 **These sentences are missing from the end of the paragraphs in Exercise 1. Write the correct letter, A–D, to say where they should go.**

a About seven of them will become deadly hurricanes. .....A......

b It threw cars and boats across the island. ....

c Not only that, the storms are getting more powerful than ever before. ....

d Ocean temperatures are getting warmer and sea levels are rising because of global warming. ....

3 **Read the report again. Write the paragraph letter next to the correct summary.**

a Definition of a hurricane. .....B..... **c** Prediction for the future. ....

b Background information. .... **d** Facts and evidence. ....

4 **Choose one of these weather events and write a similar report in your notebook.**

earthquake   flood   landslide   tsunami   typhoon   volcanic eruption

> 8.8 Poetry

1   **Read the poem aloud to yourself. What two questions does the poem ask?**

Wind On The Hill

No one can tell me,
Nobody knows,
Where the wind comes from,
Where the wind goes.

It's flying from somewhere
As fast as it can,
I couldn't keep up with it,
Not if I ran.

But if I stopped holding
The string of my kite,
It would blow with the wind
For a day and a night.

And then when I found it,
Wherever it blew,
I should know that the wind
Had been going there too.

So then I could tell them
Where the wind goes ...
But where the wind comes from
Nobody knows.

A. A. Milne

2   **Answer the questions. Write the answers in your notebook.**

a   What picture do you have in your mind after reading the poem?

b   Why is the writer fascinated by the wind?

c   Which question does the writer find the answer to?

d   What does the poem tell us about nature?

e   Try to retell the poem as a story in your own words.

9 ➤ Achievements and ambitions

➤ 9.1 I'd like to be . . .

1 Solve the crossword with names of jobs from this lesson.

Across

1 A ...... leads a team of people in an office. (7)

4 A ...... constructs buildings. (7)

7 An ...... appears in films and on the stage. (5)

11 An ...... calculates finances for businesses. (10)

12 A ...... helps make sick people well. (6)

13 A ...... looks after people when they're ill. (5)

14 A ...... repairs cars. (8)

15 A ...... works for newspapers or TV. (10)

Down

2 An ...... helps you to sell your home. (6,5)

3 A ...... puts out fires. (11)

5 An ...... designs bridges and tunnels. (8)

6 A ...... plays professional football. (10)

8 A ...... works in a laboratory. (9)

9 A ...... protects us against crime. (6,7)

10 A ...... grows plants for food. (6)

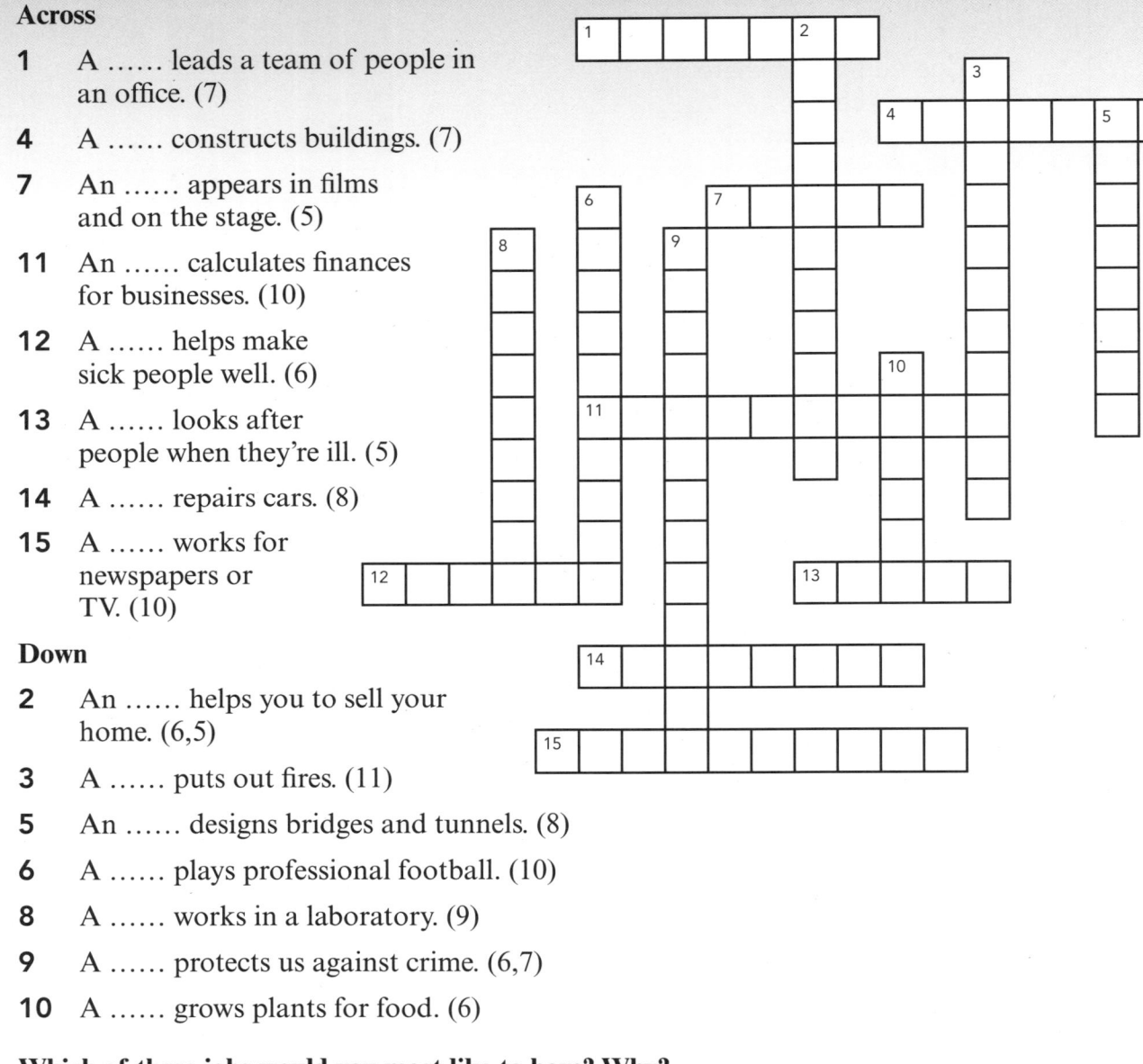

2 Which of these jobs would you most like to have? Why? Write your answer in your notebook.

> 9.2 I'm over the moon!

1 **Complete the conversation between two friends. What does Ezrine say to Aysha? For questions a–f, write the correct number 1–6.**

Aysha: Are you going to university when you finish school?

Ezrine: **a** ....

Aysha: How will you pay for the tuition fees?

Ezrine: **b** ....

Aysha: What about living costs? How will you pay for that?

Ezrine: **c** ....

Aysha: I know lots of students do that because rents are so high.

Ezrine: **d** ....

Aysha: No, how did she do that?

Ezrine: **e** ....

Aysha: And what happened?

Ezrine: **f** ....

Aysha: That's amazing!

1 Did you hear about the girl who raised money for her studies online?

2 I really hope so. If my exam results are good enough …

3 I'll need to get a student loan.

4 A famous pop star donated all the money she needed!

5 I'll probably still live at home as I can't afford to rent.

6 She set up a fundraising page on a website.

2 **Find words in the conversation to match the following definitions.**

a Money that a student can borrow from a bank. ...... *student loan* ......

b Collecting funds for a good cause. ....

c Gave money to someone who needs it. ....

d Money for accommodation and food. ....

e Not having enough money for something. ....

3 **Think about the questions. Write your answers in your notebook.**

a What are the benefits and drawbacks of getting a student loan?

b What does it mean to be socially mobile? Why is it important?

> 9.3 Would you be good at … ?

1 Match the descriptions a–f with the personal qualities 1–6.

a You've achieved a lot and been very successful. ......6......

b You're good at cooperating with a group. ....

c You're good at making decisions. ....

d People can depend on you to keep your promises. ....

e You've been familiar with computers from a young age. ....

f You are good at engaging and persuading people. ....

1 You are a digital native.

2 You have leadership qualities.

3 You have personal charm.

4 You're a team-player.

5 You're reliable.

6 Your experience is impressive.

2 Do the quiz. What personal quality do you think is the focus of each question?

> **1** Your manager at work has told you about an opportunity to go to a conference abroad. It's an exciting opportunity and you know that everyone on your team would love to go. What do you do?
> **A** Accept the offer because you think you will learn a lot.
> **B** Discuss with your team who would be the best person to attend.
> **C** Tell your team that they will get offered the opportunity next time.
>
> **2** You organised a staff meeting, but the room has been cancelled at the last minute. What do you do?
> **A** Cancel the meeting and arrange another date.
> **B** Call the building manager and complain.
> **C** Find another room and send a text with the new location.
>
> **3** You ordered some new computers for the office, but the delivery is several days late and you need them by next week. What do you do?
> **A** Cancel the order and call another company.
> **B** Call the supplier and complain.
> **C** Wait and hope that the delivery will arrive in time.
>
> Your score: **1 B** You're a good team player! **2 C** You're reliable! You don't let other people down. **3 A** You're not afraid to make decisions! You have leadership qualities.

Challenge

3 What qualities from Exercise 1 do you think you have? How do you think they will help you in a future career? Write your answers in your notebook.

> # Relative clauses

Welcome to our ice cream factory! These are the machines that we use to produce our ice cream. We have a team of experts who come up with all our flavours. The ice cream, which is sold in one-litre containers, is available for sale in our factory shop. Later we can go and sample some of the new flavours, which is the highlight of our tour!

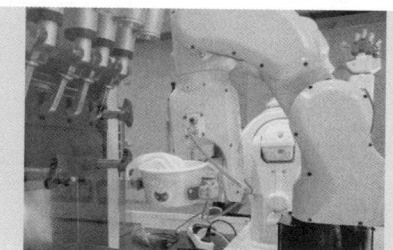

Check!

1   **Complete the rules.**

| commas   essential   non-essential   object   which |

We introduce a relative clause using a relative pronoun (*who, which* or *that*). There are two types of relative clause:

a   Those that give ....¹, defining information.

We can use *that* instead of *who* or ....² .

She is the person who (that) leads our team.

We can <u>omit</u> the relative pronoun if it refers to the ....³ of the verb.

Here is the man. I spoke to him yesterday.

He is the man (who) I spoke to yesterday.

b   Those that give extra ....⁴ information. We use ....⁵ before and after the clause and we cannot omit the pronoun.

The ice cream, which is made from organic milk, is poured into the box.

2   **Look at the picture and read the text. Underline the relative clauses. Which clauses give essential information?**

Focus

1   **Use a relative pronoun (*who, which* or *that*) to join the sentences. Which sentences need commas? Which pronouns can be omitted?**

a   This is the house. My parents designed it.

This is the house (which/that) my parents designed.

b   This is the job. I would like to apply for it.

....

c I did a part-time job last year. It was really good work experience.

....

d Here's a photo of the people. I met them at the conference.

....

e This book is really interesting. You can borrow it online.

....

f I'm going to university next year. I'm looking forward to it.

....

Practice

2 Are these sentences correct? Tick (✓) the correct sentences and correct the ones that contain errors.

a I'd really like a job*ˎ*involves working with animals, such as vet or maybe a conservationist. ☐
that

b There are a lot of people my age don't really know what kind of job they'd like to do. ☐

c My uncle's the kind of person which always takes an interest in what you're doing. ☐

d Of course, there are lots of different careers that require good communication skills. ☐

e Nowadays lots of companies employ staff which keep their social media updated. ☐

f A forensic scientist is someone which helps the police solve crimes using scientific evidence. ☐

g If you don't want to be an actor, you could be someone who works behind the scenes. ☐

h I saw a video about working in the fashion industry was really fascinating. ☐

Challenge

3 Complete the text with relative pronouns and verbs from the box.
Omit the pronoun when possible. Add commas if needed.

is	look	prefers	seem	suits	you have	you will

What kind of job would you like to have in the future? Would you like to have a job .... [1] creative, like an artist or fashion designer? Or are you someone .... [2] a reliable, secure job? Choosing a career .... [3] your talents isn't always easy. Actors and filmmakers .... [4] to have very exciting jobs can also experience a lot of stress. Some jobs .... [5] boring at first can turn out to be fascinating later on. So think carefully about the skills .... [6] and choose a career .... [7] enjoy.

⟩ Participle clauses

Rosa: How was the job fair?

Amina: It was interesting! There were dozens of companies interviewing people for jobs. I saw several managers and executives giving presentations. The people listening to the talks asked lots of questions which were really interesting. I got lots of ideas for my future career!

Check!

1 Underline the participle clauses in the dialogue.

2 Read the rules. Choose the correct words.

Participle clauses can sometimes replace relative **clauses / pronouns**[1]. They add extra information about a **verb / noun**[2]. They are often used with the **verbs / nouns**[3] of perception such as *see, watch, hear* and *notice*.

Focus

1 Which words can be deleted in each sentence?

a I saw someone ~~who was~~ running across the road.

b There were two people who were waiting outside.

c We heard a plane which was flying overhead.

d Do the keys that are lying on the floor belong to you?

e We need to find people who are working in fashion design.

Practice

2 Correct or improve these sentences using participle clauses.

a I worked for a bookshop *specialising* ~~it was specialised~~ in travel books.

b The scientists were working on the project and were told to keep it a secret.

c The candidate has the most experience would be best for the job, in my opinion.

d The estate agent that she is talking to my parents wants to sell our house.

e The manager asked the applying for the job man many questions.

Challenge

3 Complete the text with the correct form of a verb from the box.

carry	come	drive	~~run~~	stand	wear

I saw two people ....*running*........ [1] away from the bank. One man .... [2] a large bag ran into the park. The other man .... [3] a dark hat ran down a side street. Some people .... [4] near us started taking photos with their phones. Then we heard a police car .... [5] towards us. The police officer .... [6] the car stopped and asked us for a description.

Challenge

4 Think of a scene that takes place on your way to school or on your way home. Try to describe it in as much detail as you can in your notebook. Use *see*, *hear* and present participles in your description.

> ## 9.4 Achieving your dreams

1   Look at the photo and the title of the article.
     What do you think the article is about?

     ....

2   Complete the article with words from the box.

ambassadors	bare feet	champion	conflict
inspiration	marathon	Olympics	race
refugee	team		

Representing refugees
from all around the world

Yonas Kinde is an athlete from Ethiopia. He started running when he was a teenager. Following his teacher's advice, he started to run from home to school and back as practice, which was a distance of 16 kilometres each day.

He says that his .... [1] came from his idol, the Ethiopian runner Abebe Bikila, who was known for running in

.... [2] and won two Olympic gold medals for the marathon in 1960 and 1964.

After moving to Luxembourg, Yonas continued to run, and quickly became

the best .... [3] runner in

the country. He wanted to aim higher

and become a world .... [4].

However, due to his .... [5]

status, Yonas could not compete in international competitions.

On 3 July 2016, the International Olympic Committee announced that Yonas would be one of ten athletes selected to join a Refugee Olympic Athletes

.... [6]. He competed in the

men's marathon .... [7] in the

2016 Summer .... [8] in Rio

de Janeiro, finishing with a time of 2 hours 24 minutes and 8 seconds.

For young refugees across the world, sport can provide a world of hope and an

escape from .... [9]. Athletes

like Yonas are .... [10] for the power of sport to change the world. His message is: 'Sport teaches you how to win in life.'

Challenge

3   Which sportsperson or athlete do you admire? In your notebook write a short description of what makes them inspiring.

> 9.5 The power of the mind

1 Complete the sentences with words from the box.

blood pressure	blood sugar levels	chemical	immune system
~~lower~~	raise	releases	self-critical
self-esteem	visualise		

a   Exercising regularly can …*lower*… your blood pressure.

b   Doing exercise such as running can ………………………… your heart rate.

c   Your ………………………… helps your body fight off infections.

d   Stress and anxiety can lead to high …………………………

e   Lack of insulin can lead to high …………………………

f   Dopamine is a ………………………… that helps our brains to function.

g   Your body ………………………… insulin in response to rising sugar levels in your blood.

h   Your ………………………… is your evaluation of yourself. It can be low or high!

i   If you are …………………………, it means you tend to evaluate yourself negatively.

j   If you ………………………… something, you see it in your mind's eye and imagine it is real.

2 Rewrite the questions using the words from Exercise 1.

a   What can you do to think more positively about yourself?

What can you do to ……… *improve your self-esteem* …………?

b   How can you learn not to criticise yourself too much?

How can you learn ……………………………………?

c   How can you help to make your dreams a reality?

How can you ……………………………………?

d   How can you fight off infections more easily?

How can you strengthen ……………………………………?

e   What can you do to reduce stress and anxiety?

What can you do to ……………………………………?

3 Answer the questions in Exercise 2. Write your ideas in your notebook.

❯ 9.6 Young achievers

1   **Match the definitions with the words in the box.**

brave	capable	confident	creative
curious	determined	fearless	intelligent
~~ambitious~~	inventive	optimistic	skilful

a   You dream of being a famous writer or a world champion! .... *ambitious* ....

b   You're willing to work hard, overcome obstacles and never give up. ....

c   You're afraid of nothing and you are brave in difficult situations. ....

d   You think positively about the future. ....

e   You are fascinated by everything and always want to learn more. ....

f   You're good at learning new things and can solve problems easily. ....

g   You come up with original new ideas. ....

h   Whatever task you are given, you manage it efficiently and well. ....

i   You're good at doing many different kinds of things. ....

j   You have a lot of imagination and are good at art, design and writing. ....

k   You are sure of yourself in a positive and realistic way. ....

l   You are ready to face dangerous or difficult situations. ....

2   **What qualities are important for each job? Write three different adjectives from Exercise 1 for each one.**

Firefighter	Surgeon	Athlete	Artist

Challenge

3   **Which adjectives describe you best? Write a paragraph in your notebook.**

> Reported speech – statements (revision)

Use of English

Check!

In reported statements, we change the tense of the original statement, so that it is one tense further back.

Complete the tense changes.

present simple → past simple

present continuous → ....

present perfect → ....

past continuous → ....

will → ....

We change pronouns so that they are seen from the reporter's point of view.

'I phoned you' → She said she had phoned me.

We change time reference words, so they are seen from a later point of time.

It's been a dream of ours to win this championship and I am proud of our achievement.

The captain said it had been a dream of theirs to win this championship and she was proud of their achievement.

'I'll see you tomorrow' → She said she would see me the next day.

tonight → that night   tomorrow → the next day   yesterday → the day before
last year → the year before   next week → the following week

Focus

1   **Read the caption near the picture. What differences are there between the original statement and the reported statement?**

   ....

   ....

2   **Complete the reported statements.**

   a   'I want to compete in the Olympics next year,' she said.

      She said ....*she*.... wanted to compete in the Olympics ..*the following year*..

b 'We're going to start training next week,' they said.

They said .... were going to start training ....

c 'It's been a dream of mine since I was a child,' he said.

He said it had been a dream of .... since .... was a child.

d 'I'll tell you my news tomorrow,' she told us.

She told us .... would tell .... news ....

e 'I didn't want to be late yesterday,' she told them.

She said ....

Practice

3 **Choose the correct option to complete the reported statements.**

a 'At the moment, we're slightly behind the training schedule.'

Last week, he told me *they're / they were* slightly behind the training schedule.

b 'Maria's started playing on the team.'

Amy said that Maria *was started / had started* playing on the team.

c 'Surprise! We're going to Dubai!'

She only told me where *we're going / we were going* when we got to the airport!

d 'You'll need to train really hard.'

When I joined the club, my coach said *I'll need / I'd need* to train hard.

e 'I was cycling home from school when I saw the accident.'

So, you said you *cycled / were cycling* home from school when you saw the accident.

Challenge

4 **Rewrite each person's statements as reported speech in your notebook.**

a **Kemal:** I've been training for the marathon for five years. I won my first race last year. It was an amazing experience. My family are really proud.

b **Joanna:** I started to do judo last year. I've learned so much from my teammates! I'm going to start entering competitions next year. I'm hoping to be a world champion one day.

c **Kara and Makoto:** We started our own football team this year. We're playing our first big match tomorrow. We're really excited about it!

> Dependent prepositions following adjectives

Use of English

Safia: Are you worried about something?

Omar: I'm nervous about doing my music exam tomorrow.

Safia: Was your teacher satisfied with your level?

Omar: Yes, but I'm scared of letting her down.

Check!

1   **Read the conversation above. Underline the adjectives that are followed by a preposition. Circle the prepositions.**

2   **Add the adjectives in the box to the list below.**

bored	famous	polite	proud	worried

Some adjectives are followed by certain prepositions.
It can be useful to group adjectives with the same preposition together.

+ about   nervous, ...[1], concerned, anxious, angry, annoyed, upset, excited

+ to   good, kind, nice, ...[2], grateful, thankful, similar

+ for   good, bad, ...[3], grateful, thankful, sorry

+ with   satisfied, familiar, pleased, happy, ...[4], fed up

+ of   ....[5], afraid, scared, frightened, capable

- Some adjectives are followed by more than one preposition.

- We can be angry **about** something, but angry **with** someone.

- Someone can be good **to** you. Too much sugar isn't good **for** you.

- Remember that a preposition is followed by a noun or an *-ing* form.

Focus

1   **Choose the correct word.**

a   Sara is nervous *about* / *of* / *from* playing in the competition tomorrow.

b   These vitamins are really good *to* / *for* / *with* you.

c   Are you pleased *of* / *at* / *with* your team's performance?

d   I'm proud *to* / *of* / *with* my sister for winning the prize.

e We're very grateful *to / for / about* all your help.

f My sister's really afraid *of / at / from* spiders.

Practice

2 Complete the sentences so they are appropriate for the context.

a Your friend comes to visit unexpectedly and your room is a mess.

'I'm sorry ....*about the mess*.........'

b You're talking about the health benefits of swimming.

'Swimming is really good ....'

c Your brother has done something that's made you angry.

'I'm really angry ....,'

d You're late handing in your homework.

'I'm sorry .... delay.'

e Your paintings skills aren't great.

'I'm not very good ....,'

Challenge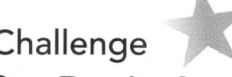

3 Rewrite these sentences in your notebook using the underlined adjective and a preposition.
Use an *-ing* form if necessary.

a You came to our concert! We're <u>grateful</u>!

   We're grateful to you for coming to our concert.

b I've got a maths test tomorrow. I'm <u>worried</u>.

c They make delicious biscuits in my home town. That's why it is <u>famous</u>.

d I'm so late! I'm <u>sorry</u>!

e I have to give a presentation tomorrow. I'm not sure if I'm <u>capable</u>.

f My brother took my phone. I'm really <u>angry</u>!

⊙ Get it right!

Remember that some adjectives are used with different prepositions depending on the context.

- **sorry about / for** + noun / -ing – used to apologise when you are responsible
  We are **sorry for** *the inconvenience caused to passengers.* (more formal)
  I'm really **sorry about** *the mess – my dad's painting the house.* (more informal)

- **sorry about** + noun – you feel bad about a situation you are not responsible for
  I'm **sorry about** *your trip being cancelled – that's so annoying.* ✓
  I'm **sorry for** *your trip being cancelled – that's so annoying.* ✗

- **good at** something – have skill / ability
  You need to be quite **good at** *maths to become a scientist.* ✓
  You need to be quite **good in** *maths to become a scientist.* ✗

- **good for** someone / something – have advantages / benefits
  More people walking and cycling would be **good for** *the environment.*

- **good to** someone – kind to them
  She was really **good to** *me when I broke my leg and couldn't get out.*

> 9.7 Improve your writing

1 **Read the letter from Kwame to himself. What is the purpose of the letter? Tick (✓) the correct answer.**

☐ To give himself some advice

☐ To reflect on what he has learned

☐ To explain how he has changed

Dear Kwame,

You are starting a new school year. It's a very important time in your life. You're going to learn a lot of new subjects and you'll make new friends. .... [1]

The most important thing is to be yourself. .... [2] Be brave and stand up for your own opinions and what you think is right.

Secondly, always do your best and don't skip any lessons or homework. .... [3] This is the time to try out new things and discover your talents. Be ambitious, but also be realistic.

Thirdly, don't be discouraged if you make mistakes or get a bad exam result. .... [4] That is how people learn to succeed and that will help you to follow your dreams.

Good luck on your future path!

Kwame

---

2 **Read the letter again. Where do the missing sentences go?**

a Don't try to copy others or let anyone bully you.

b Here is some advice for you that I learned during this past school year.

c Pick yourself up and try again!

d Work hard and be curious.

3 **How did you feel at the start of the school year? Tick (✓) the statements that are true for you.**

☐ I felt nervous about meeting new classmates.

☐ I was worried I wouldn't have any friends.

☐ I hoped that the teachers would not be too strict.

☐ I wanted to be the best in the class.

☐ I wasn't sure if I was capable of doing all the work.

4 **Make notes about yourself in your notebook using the topics above. Use your notes to write a letter to yourself at the start of this school year.**

> 9.8 Fiction

1 Read the extract from Chapter 11 of *Rickshaw Girl* by Mitali Perkins. This extract describes Naima's first meeting with the owner of the rickshaw repair shop.

> Naima's head whirled and her mouth fell open. This widow was the owner of a rickshaw repair shop? Here–in a village just like her own? How could that be? But the woman had half-turned to see her, and that was a brush in her hand. That was paint staining her *saree*. Naima hadn't noticed the shining rectangle of unpainted tin propped up in front of her.
>
> "My first order, and only one day to complete it," the woman was saying, almost as if she were talking to herself. "I need to concentrate, and all I get are interruptions." She didn't bother keeping the irritation out of her voice.
>
> Naima didn't move. The woman made an exasperated noise and went back to work. Naima peered over her shoulder as the woman dipped the brush in a pot of yellow paint. The slim, stained fingers guided the brush, leaving a trail of yellow leaves across the tin.
>
> "I could help you," Naima said suddenly. "I paint the best *alpanas* in my village."

2 Answer the questions.

a What two things is Naima surprised by?

....

....

b What is "the shining rectangle of unpainted tin"?

....

c What is the woman doing?

....

d Why is the woman annoyed?

....

e What personal qualities does Naima demonstrate when she says, "I could help you. I paint the best *alpanas* in my village"? Write two ideas.

....

3 What does this extract tell us about how to achieve our dreams?

....

....